T0231545

Practical Data Security

UNICOM
Applied Information Technology

edited by
John Gordon

Routledge
Taylor & Francis Group

LONDON AND NEW YORK

First published 1993 by Ashgate Publishing

Reissued 2018 by Routledge
2 Park Square, Milton Park, Abingdon, Oxon OX14 4RN
711 Third Avenue, New York, NY 10017, USA

Routledge is an imprint of the Taylor & Francis Group, an informa business

Copyright © UNICOM Seminars Ltd 1993

Chapter 2 © Crown copyright 1992. Published with the permission of the controller of Her Majesty's Stationery Office. The views expressed are those of the authors and do not necessarily reflect those of the Department of Trade and Industry or any other Government Department.

All rights reserved. No part of this book may be reprinted or reproduced or utilised in any form or by any electronic, mechanical, or other means, now known or hereafter invented, including photocopying and recording, or in any information storage or retrieval system, without permission in writing from the publishers.

Notice:
Product or corporate names may be trademarks or registered trademarks, and are used only for identification and explanation without intent to infringe.

Publisher's Note
The publisher has gone to great lengths to ensure the quality of this reprint but points out that some imperfections in the original copies may be apparent.

Disclaimer
The publisher has made every effort to trace copyright holders and welcomes correspondence from those they have been unable to contact.

A Library of Congress record exists under LC control number : 93001531

ISBN 13: 978-1-138-33098-6 (hbk)
ISBN 13: 978-0-429-44747-1 (ebk)

Contents

Data Security – An Introduction

John Gordon
Concept Laboratories

Between about the years 1900 and 1975 over 50 per cent of workers in the developed world were manufacturing physical goods. Since that time most people now generate or process information.

This is a revolution which has crept up on us. We have become accustomed to our bank accounts, our airline bookings, our medical and employment records all being managed by computers. Processing power is now so cheap that in the world ahead virtually everything will be carried out by computer. Even now advanced design is carried out by CAD, advanced manufacture by programmed machine, and advanced aircraft are flown by computer.

Since these machines will one day control almost all aspects of our lives, it is pertinent to ask to what degree we can trust them. We would like to know how reliable they are. In large systems consisting of a mixture of manual and automated processes, we are interested in failure modes and their knock-on consequences to the organisation. We are also interested in what we can do to prevent these things, to lessen the consequences, or to recover from them. These are all data security issues.

Data security is emerging as one of the fastest growing areas in the IT revolution. It is concerned with ensuring that computer systems provide properly understood and controlled benefits, and that their design and installation and the applications and data which run on them are put together in such a way that catastrophes are made as rare and survivable as possible.

This discipline is not growing in isolation. It can be viewed as part of a trend towards quality in general. This trend includes the moves towards adopting quality standards, health and safety standards, and so forth.

This book is a collection of papers, many of which were presented at a seminar in London in 1992 [1], and which together form an excellent treatment by leading experts in some of the key areas of current concern in data security. This introduction reviews the subject as a whole.

WHAT IS DATA SECURITY?

Data security is concerned with protecting the confidentiality, integrity and availability of the IT assets of an organisation.

Its IT assets consist of everything an organisation needs to generate, store, process, transmit and output its records and data. Included are personnel, mainframe and personal computers, databases, printers, networks, and so forth.

Most companies employing more than a handful of people are today critically dependent on their records. While many organisations could survive loss of buildings and plant, almost none could ever recover from the loss of its records. Even a temporary loss of access to its data resources for as little as forty-eight hours is enough to wreck a major financial institution.

INFORMATION

Information is unlike matter or energy. It can be both created and destroyed. It can be copied. It can be memorised. It is undeniably an abstraction, but nevertheless we live and die by it.

Money itself is but a form of information. Accountancy is in a sense a discipline attempting the artificial imposition on money of certain laws akin to the physical law of conservation of matter.

The strange properties of information mean special problems in securing it.

CONFIDENTIALITY, INTEGRITY, AVAILABILITY

Specialists recognise three qualities as being fundamental to data security. These are *confidentiality, integrity* and *availability.*

Confidentiality (secrecy) is the traditional and original security discipline. It is of greatest concern to the old-school security community consisting of the military, the secret services, the police and the diplomatic corps. For these people secrecy was traditionally paramount. They use a collection of security paradigms such as the *Need to Know Principle* – a rule for dissemination of information which says that data shall be withheld if the potential recipient does not have a compelling and positive need for it.

Confidentiality is lost if data is disclosed, either deliberately or accidentally. To state the obvious, when information leaks out the original is usually still in place. Information does not obey conservation laws and – even worse – there may not even be a record of its leaking out. Moreover it cannot be collected and put back.

Security measures to protect confidentiality include cryptography and access control.

Integrity is about being sure of the correctness, consistency and timeliness of information. In other words integrity is about the meaning of the data, and about it being fit for the purpose for which it was intended. Integrity may be lost if data is badly managed, or it may be lost as a result of a deliberate attack. A malfunctioning computer program can lose, in a few seconds, the integrity of records which have taken years to amass. For example, a bug in a newly developed application can wreck the data fed into it. Faulty manual procedures can result in data being damaged from the moment it is captured. Certain viruses can wreak havoc with data.

Integrity is protected by backups, operating procedures, access control, and audit, as well as by certain aspects of cryptography.

Availability is about being sure that data is accessible when it is needed, where it is needed. Even though data is intact and confidential it can still lose availability. Availability is lost if a computer centre, a key network component, or even a power supply breaks down, or if a building needs to be evacuated. Of course availability is also lost if the data itself is lost or destroyed or its integrity is lost. Availability is protected by standby facilities, backups, fire precautions, disaster recovery procedures and so forth.

It is common practice to classify all disasters under one or more of the three headings – confidentiality, integrity and availability – rather than inventing new headings. For example, political embarrassment might be regarded as one of the more serious dangers in certain organisations, but this can usually be traced to loss of confidentiality.

Data security is unusual among management disciplines for the sheer number of areas upon which it impacts. To have adequate data security an organisation needs to pay particular attention to its policy regarding:

- personnel;
- buildings;
- choice of site;
- insurance;
- training;
- communication networks;
- accounting;
- auditing;
- data processing;
- data storage;
- health and safety policy;
- legislation;
- standards.

HOW TO BE SECURE

The sensible way to handle risk is to have a *Security Policy*. The policy in turn should be based on a study of the issues involved. The most appropriate type of study, is called a *Risk Analysis*. Knowing the risks, the board of directors can then make decisions about what to do about the risks. They may, in the light of the study decide to live with the risk. Or at the other extreme they may decide to take every known precaution, including an appropriate *training* program, a comprehensive set of *countermeasures* including cryptography and access control, a contingency and disaster recovery plan, a personnel policy, a physical security policy, a policy on PC and network security, a large measure of insurance cover, and so forth.

Implementation of this policy may require the purchase of specialist products and services, which in turn requires determining their suitability for the purpose. Recent moves towards international standardization under the term ITSEC (for 'IT Security Evaluation Criteria') [2] are aimed at precisely this area.

SECURITY POLICY

Security is in a class along with health-and-safety, and quality. These activities all cost money and effort; they are perceived by some people, often erroneously, as interfering with and disrupting the main business of the organisation, and they may therefore suffer when competing for resources against the needs of productivity and profit.

Under UK law at least, the responsibility for the security of the IT assets of a company (its databases, networks, mainframes etc.) does not reside with the DP department, nor with the communications department, nor even with the security manager. It is the company directors who are responsible, and indeed *personally* responsible, for the security of these assets.

Security measures might never be undertaken by a workforce unless some coercion were applied, and it is up to company directors to provide the framework and the impetus. Only company directors have the power to enforce security procedures upon a workforce. Without active and unequivocal backing from the board of directors all security procedures are doomed.

Since a company director is not normally an expert on security, this area is properly covered by an appropriate security policy.

Apart from the legal responsibility, it makes good sense to have a clear policy on security. Such a policy can help to:

- ensure that uniform standards are applied, and that no loopholes are knowingly left;
- permit cost-effectiveness considerations to enter the discussion in a controlled way;
- make clear the management's views on security;
- provide a basis for answering questions on security matters.

RISK ANALYSIS AND MANAGEMENT

As we have said, the responsibility for taking care of data assets falls personally on the shoulders of the organisation's directors. It therefore behooves them to ensure that they are taking all reasonable precautions and are behaving in a way which is manifestly responsible.

A properly carried out, thorough risk analysis will provide a professional, considered, and definitive statement of the risks to which the enterprise is subject, plus recommendations regarding the proper courses of action. Provided that a director adheres to most of these recommendations he could probably defend himself against a charge of negligence.

Of all the measures an organisation can take when it first becomes aware of the need for a policy on data security, probably the one which should be undertaken first is a thorough risk analysis.

Risk analysis shows the size and nature of the problem. It provides a baseline measurement of the state of risk to which an organisation is exposed – a basis from which to select controls.

Risk management (as opposed to risk analysis) is concerned with actually doing something about the risks which come to light as a result of a risk analysis study. Often the two are linked together under any of a number of titles including: Risk Analysis, Risk Management, Risk Analysis and Management, Risk Management Program, Risk Methodology, or similar combinations.

Risk analysis is to data security as market research is to business. Both are:

- a good starting point;
- a basis for other activities;
- an inexact pseudo-science;
- concerned with planning, consistency and coordination.

In other words it is a valuable if inexact measuring tool, best used up front before carrying out other activities.

Risk analysis is a type of research which tells you about the state of risk of your business in relation to industry norms. It provides an overview of the exposure of data assets to various catastrophes. Together with a program of risk management it can help to ensure that the true risks are properly protected by a coherent, coordinated policy, that resources are concentrated where they are needed, and that money is not wasted protecting low-value or easily replaced assets or on countermeasures which will not be effective.

Properly carried out, a risk management program can save not only a great deal of risk but a great deal of money. Some large organisations save many times more money in reduced insurance premiums than they spend in risk management.

Also a risk analysis may reveal that some countermeasures would be a waste of money. For example it may be found on analysis that an expensive, permanent, cold-standby site would not bring the operation back on-line quickly enough to save the business. This money was therefore being wasted.

As well as being applicable on an enterprise-wide basis, risk analysis can be applied to individual projects. Enlightened organisations regard a proper risk analysis as an integral part of the lifecycle of each project.

DISASTER RECOVERY AND CONTINGENCY PLANNING

The majority of companies which rely on data processing could not survive the loss of availability of this resource for more than a few days. Most of these companies have no budget for disaster recovery, and only about one in three has any kind of plan in place.

The main concepts in the domain of disaster recovery and contingency planning are the notions of contingency, contingency planning, continuity planning, survival planning and disaster recovery planning. Authors are not unanimous on the meanings of these terms, but the following is a rough guide.

The possibility of occurrence *in the future* of damaging events, accidents or disasters, of which the exact nature and timing cannot be known at the present time is called a *Contingency*. A *Contingency Plan* is a set of measures aimed at dealing with such unforeseen events when they take place. A *Continuity Plan* is an outline of strategies and actions needed to reduce the likelihood of disasters occurring and keeping the operation going. This term also includes survival planning, disaster recovery planning etc. It is a generic term to encompass all activities which allow an organisation to continue doing business. A *Survival Plan* is a set of measures to be implemented immediately after a contingency to help reduce the initial impact. A *Disaster Recovery Plan* is a plan which concentrates on the recovery of the data processing and computer system facilities.

CRYPTOGRAPHY

The study of cryptography ('secret codes') was until recently limited to the protection solely of confidentiality, and was the domain of the military and the secret services.

Now the subject has blossomed to become one of the more sophisticated and scientific tools of data security. Its uses are now far wider than the mere protection of confidentiality.

Cryptographic methods can now:

- prevent or detect attempts to repudiate an agreement or contract;
- guarantee the authenticity of a message;
- determine whether a payment is fresh, or is a recording of an earlier payment;
- prevent masquerade;
- prevent undetected deletion of messages;
- prevent undetected alteration of data;
- prevent unauthorised, meaningful changes to data;
- prevent message-rerouting;
- prevent statistical analysis of traffic;
- prevent injection of unauthorised messages.

We now include under the general heading of cryptography recent methods to guarantee the authenticity of documents, to prevent repudiation of authorship, of document certification, and of personal identification.

Conventional cryptography (for confidentiality) involves *encryption* of data, which means transforming the symbols comprising it by an essentially mathematical procedure under the control of a special parameter called the *key*. This process renders the resulting *ciphertext* meaningless to anyone who does not possess knowledge of the key. The ciphertext is then transmitted or stored, and subsequently *decrypted* by means of an appropriate key.

By far the greatest problem with running a cryptographically secure network is the *key management* in a real operational environment.

These are some of the issues in key management:
- keys must be kept secret – not just before use but afterwards too – since otherwise an enemy can stockpile ciphertext for later decryption;
- any weakness in the mechanism used to transmit keys is far more serious than a weakness in transmitting data, since compromise of a key compromises all the data encrypted with it;
- keys must be changed frequently enough – both in terms of time and usage – to satisfy security requirements;

• loss of keys by legitimate users results in loss of data. Accordingly there is a need for key backup. This of course increases the problems of key confidentiality.

Altogether, and despite some very ingenious techniques, there remain a number of serious operational problems which require managerial solutions. This is a very big subject.

Cryptography is probably the most technically complex of all the disciplines in data security. To understand the issues requires mastery of mathematics and computational complexity theory.

However in practice its benefits are many, and sophisticated products are readily available off the shelf.

ACCESS CONTROL

Access control is different from other security measures in that it attempts to prevent attacks at the source, thereby winning the battle before it starts.

Access control is concerned with:

• identifying people attempting access;
• determining whether they have entitlement to access;
• maintaining a record of accesses.

Key concepts in access control are:

• *Identification*
The control system must know who it is dealing with before it can make a decision whether to permit access.Identification can use passwords, tokens or smart cards, or it can operate by attempting some form of pattern recognition on the person ('biometrics'). The latter might include fingerprint or handwriting recognition.
• *Authorization*
The control system must have decision rules to be able to authorize access to valid users.
• *Audit*
When a log of accesses and access attempts is kept, it is called an Audit. The log is part of an *Audit Trail* and normally includes the times and dates of valid, and especially invalid, attempts at access.

ITSEC – IT SECURITY AND EVALUATION CRITERIA

Security products can be very expensive and make no direct, extra profit for the customer. Often it is necessary to buy hundreds of the same product to ensure coverage across all branches of a business. Any unforseen security weakness which comes to light after purchase and installation is very disheartening.

However it is notoriously difficult for customers to evaluate hardware and software products intended for security applications. There are a number of reasons for this:

- In looking for weaknesses in a security product, what one is interested in is not absence of any evidence that it has a weakness, but rather *evidence of the absence of any weaknesses*. One would like to be able to show that there *cannot exist* any sequence of legal operations which would result in a security breach.
- When a skilled opponent attacks security countermeasures he will often attempt an indirect approach using lateral thinking. It is not just the normal operation of the security system which matters but also its performance 'under fire'.
- Security claims are often very technical and full of jargon.
- Many security products are complex microprocessor-controlled subsystems with very intricate software. It is often almost impossible to check out all conceivable operating circumstances.
- Manufacturers may make claims for the security of systems which are ambiguous, hard to understand, or simply untrue.

Against this background the governments of France, Germany, the Netherlands and the UK collaborated in a program called ITSEC (for IT Security Evaluation Criteria) [2], with a view to harmonising evaluation criteria for security products. Version 1.2 appeared in June 1991 with further issues to follow. The purpose of this exercise is to provide 'assurance of the correctness or the effectiveness of security-enforcing functions'. ITSEC defines a number of security profiles, together with an accreditation scheme for products.

There is widespread but qualified support for this work. From the manufacturer's standpoint the accreditation process is extremely long-winded and costly. From the customer's standpoint ITSEC may not necessarily address the issues which are his direct concern, and it certainly drives up the price of the products. However it is a move in the right direction, and it is here to stay.

PERSONNEL

Most of the deliberate damage to IT assets is not carried out by hackers or outsiders but by the employees of the victim organisation themselves. Mistakes in the selection process of employees can prove to be costly both financially and to the image and reputation of the company.

Examples of hostile activities undertaken by employees include: selling information to competitors; theft of company property; introduction of viruses into company computers; destruction or corruption of company records and data, e.g. by *logical timebombs*; and the destruction and sabotage of company equipment. Personnel-generated losses may not solely be the result of deliberate hostile activity. Many problems are merely accidents or operator errors, for which training may be the appropriate remedy.

A personnel policy, which covers data security must address:

- recruitment;
- training;
- supervision;
- appraisal;
- statutory leave;
- separation of duties;
- job rotation;
- duplication of expertise;
- termination.

PHYSICAL SECURITY

For certain threats the physical security of a company is its first line of defence.

Physical security measures protect not only against planned attacks but also against natural disasters which could seriously jeopardise a company's future. While access control covers many of these issues, there are others which are normally termed physical security. The relevant areas of concern are:

Site
- location
- neighbouring hazards
- security

Buildings
- construction
- layout
- security

Fire protection
- training

Flood protection

Electromagnetic emanations
- from power lines
- from transmitters

Disposal of waste
- facilities for disposing of sensitive materials such as printer ribbons, disks, documents etc.

The following is a sample of the considerations affecting data security which come under the heading of physical security.

- Is the site located in a valley where there may be a danger of flooding? If this is the case, then it is possible that operations will be affected, disabling the company's data processing capability.

- Is the location prone to earthquakes? Earthquakes can cause major structural damage to the building and endanger lives. In the event of a serious earthquake it is inevitable that the data processing capabilities of the company will be affected, with a long delay before the situation can be remedied.

- Is there a danger of forest fires in the vicinity? In some countries forest fires, as well as fires to neighbouring buildings, can cause disruption through evacuation of personnel and shutting down of operations.

- Are there dangers from the neighbours? Neighbouring companies and other establishments (e.g. power stations) may also constitute threats. Examples are nuclear reactors, chemical processing plants and prisons. Problems in these establishments may require the evacuation or other disruptions of the surrounding area.

- Is it possible to secure the perimeter of the site? This may not be possible if there is a public right-of-way through the site. It may be necessary to install surveillance equipment to monitor the perimeter of the site against intruders.

- Is the site situated within easy reach of the emergency services? This could make the difference between life or death in the event of a disaster such as fire.

- Does the site have a history of problems? It may be the case that the site has been prone to attacks or criminal damage in the past, making it more likely to be attacked in the future.
- A building of sound construction is more likely to survive a disaster.
- The location and design of windows can stop intruders from breaking in. If there is sensitive work to be done within the building it makes sense not to allow people to spy through the windows.
- The safe location of vital functions within the building can reduce the likelihood of excessive damage in the event of a disaster. For example, it would not be good practice to locate the data processing centre in the basement where it would be at most danger from flooding
- Splitting the internal layout of the building into different security zones can help in increasing access control to vital functions which can be grouped together and sectioned off from the rest of the building, with access to them carefully controlled. The whole building can be zoned, with each zone having varying security controls. Personnel may be excluded from sensitive parts of the building without proper authorization.
- No smoking rules can dramatically reduce the risks of fire within the company.
- Clearly marked fire-fighting equipment present within the building, and staff trained to use such equipment, can prevent small incidents from developing into large scale catastrophes.
- Within the data processing centre, reliable automatic fire detecting and extinguishing equipment, in the form of Halon gas, can minimise the risk of damage to expensive equipment. Non-flammable materials employed within the building wherever possible can reduce the extent to which, and the speed at which, fire can spread.

VIRUSES

A computer virus is a deliberately constructed computer program which has two characteristics:

- it makes copies of itself and spreads from system to system;
- it has a *mission* which may include inflicting damage on the system which hosts it.

The term 'virus' is chosen because of the uncanny similarity to biological viruses.

A virus has the ability to reproduce itself and spread from one system to another. It does this by copying itself onto any floppy diskettes it encounters, or via a network. This phase usually carries on for a long period ('incubation period'), perhaps months, before the virus announces its presence by carrying out its mission. The mission is some damaging or threatening action. The action may be merely a token gesture – for example the displaying of a provocative message on the screen – but it could be much more serious.

Non-destructive viruses are practical jokes in poor taste. They are probably not intended to do any real harm. Well-known examples include *Stoned, Search* and *IBM Xmas Tree.* They usually display a message following some trigger.

Destructive viruses are written with the intent to cause damage – typically, deletion of files and reformatting of disks. Examples are *Datacrime, Michaelangelo, Friday 13th* and *Jerusalem.*

It is possible to detect and eliminate them by various technical and operational methods.

PC AND NETWORK SECURITY

The majority of information processing done within many companies is now often distributed rather than central. This is largely due to the increase in power of PCs and workstations, and to the increasing tendency to network them together. In most cases the total distributed processing power within an organisation (PCs and workstations) is far greater than that of a large mainframe.

All the IT security considerations for stand-alone computers apply to networks and, in addition, networks have some special problems all their own.

Networks form a way for an attacker to penetrate a computer system without needing physical access. Attacks can even come from abroad where the laws are different and where the attacker is safe from recrimination. It is possible to transfer funds by network so fast that the equivalent of the entire Gross National Product (GNP) of a nation could be sent abroad in minutes.

One of the best protections for networks is cryptography. This can protect confidentiality and also ensure that it is impossible to alter or inject messages without detection.

There are whole networks consisting almost entirely of PCs. This development stems directly from the PC revolution – the rapid growth in popularity of PCs, which has fed on, and simultaneously contributed to, the low cost of these devices. The key features contributing to the almost universal use of PCs are precisely the same ones which make them highly insecure. A PC can be described as a filing cabinet with a built-in photocopier, allowing the theft of documents with the originals remaining in place.

The risks to PCs range from simple misuse, software piracy, and viruses, to the more serious theft or destruction of vital data.

There are devices on the market which can help to implement security controls on PCs. Add-on hardware and software is available which can, to a greater or lesser extent, control access to the PC.

Disk encryption devices allow all of the data exchange between the PC and its disks to be encrypted. A password is required upon system bootup, this forms part of the encryption/decryption key. The encryption/decryption is done in hardware on a plug-in card which replaces the normal hard disk controller.

There is a wide range of encryption devices to provide network security.

INSURANCE

Some data security controls work by lessening the probability of a threat, while others aim to reduce the vulnerability to threats; some attempt to detect a threat in the early stages, while others are designed to limit the magnitude of any resulting security breach; then there are some which make provision to recover from the damage of a security breach.

However, there is one control which does none of these. Insurance is about getting someone else to bear the risk on your behalf – for a fee.

A security policy may simply be not to attempt to protect against certain threats because they are not regarded as likely enough to justify expensive controls, or because the controls required might be too inconvenient or disruptive to the main business of the organisation.

Under these or other circumstances a degree of protection can be provided against some remaining threats through proper insurance.

Insurance is not a substitute for loss prevention and disaster recovery planning. It is a conscious step in the full light of knowledge of the risks involved. It should be part of a security policy, a decision to subcontract some of the consequences of potential losses to the insurer.

At the risk of stating the obvious, the benefit of insurance to the insured is that it will provide funds to reduce the financial impact of a loss from a disaster – it will not actually reduce the likelihood of loss, nor the extent of the loss when it occurs. Only proper countermeasures can do these things.

Having said this, nothing is of course quite that simple. Insurance is not completely independent of precautions since the insurance company will base its premiums largely on its perceptions of the risks involved, which in turn will depend to a large extent on the precautions.

Moreover, an organisation with a poor track record on security incidents, or an irresponsible attitude to risks, may find that no insurance company is willing to bear the risks for any price.

The issues concerned with insurance are many and complex.

LEGISLATION

When the United Kingdom Data Protection act was first discussed some argued that computer data was in principle no different from that stored in filing cabinets – it is just quicker and easier to access more data on computers. By this argument a pistol differs from a peashooter only in muzzle velocity. The reality is that when a difference in magnitude is sufficiently large it becomes a *de facto* difference in kind.

Computers pose special problems for legislators, among them:

- The ease with which data may be copied is a great temptation to many people. Even some well respected organisations have been known to order fewer copies of software than are actually in use.
- To effect damage to a database on a massive scale does not require a commensurate effort. It is sufficient to instruct a computer to do the damage.
- Tracking criminals and proving their crimes to the satisfaction of a judge and jury can be not only extremely difficult but highly technical. Attackers can go to great lengths to cover their tracks and confuse the issues. There are difficulties in getting a jury to understand what has been committed.
- There is no long-standing history of social abhorrence of computer crime. Hackers have been heros in movies and society does not perceive them as evil. Computer criminals may have a university education and usually do not fit the popular stereotype of a villain.

In the UK the recent acts of most concern to IT security are the

- Data Protection Act 1984, and the
- Computer Misuse Act 1990.

The Data Protection Act is concerned with protecting the rights of individuals who are the subjects of stored data, while the Computer Misuse Act is concerned with protecting the owners of stored data from attacks on that data.

REFERENCES

[1] *Practical Data Security, Risks, Costs and Solutions*, Seminar at London Heathrow Hilton, June 30-July 1, 1992. Unicom Seminars, Uxbridge, Middlesex, UB8 3PH, England.

[2] *Information Technology Security Evaluation Criteria (ITSEC)*, Luxembourg: Office for Official Publications of the European Communities, 1991, Cat. Num. CD-71-91-502-EN-C.

1 An Organisation for Security in a Major Company

Charles Brookson
British Telecom

1.1 BACKGROUND

Some years ago our main concerns within the company were with the investigation and detection of crime, with national security and to a lesser extent commercial security.

On becoming a commercial concern instead of a public utility, it became clear that proactive working had many more benefits than the reactive style. This has led to the introduction of units responsible for crime prevention, advice and electronic security. Over the years we have changed into our present organisation which has been modelled to meet the business's needs, and in 1991 a major reorganisation took place to formalise the changes.

1.2 THE BUSINESS JUSTIFICATION

The motivation for good security comes from the concern for quality, to save on the costs of security failures, and good business practice.

The most easily identifiable motivating reason is that of cost. Many security failures will inflict a direct cost on the customer, network or system, for example by gaining the power to make free calls or access to services, or by the theft of physical assets or goods.

Another area of concern is the theft of information which may lead to a commercial advantage to a competitor, such as the knowledge of new techniques, intellectual property, or marketing information from our customer base. The most important values are integrity, availability, and confidentiality of the information.

Of concern to the Company are some of the indirect consequential losses resulting from a security failure. These costs are harder to quantify and so are not often taken into account when deciding a security strategy. They include:

- investigation time, that is the time spent by experts to determine the scope of and put right any failure;

- loss of time for people, and the consequential problems of people being unable to fulfil their normal jobs;

- data destruction or lack of data integrity where it is impossible to recover data;

- legal implications, where external legal obligations are placed on us, such as the Data Protection Act, our licence conditions, and the Financial Services Act.

Other reasons that may lead to security being considered are:

- loss of customer confidence, where a security failure causes a customer to look elsewhere for the service; and

- indirect losses such as contracts and similar penalties, where a penalty results for late delivery or similar obligations under the contract.

1.3 ORGANISATION OF THE SECURITY WITHIN THE COMPANY

A high visibility of the importance of security is necessary within a company. It is important that all people at senior levels are aware of the problems and risks, and also behave and act in a way that strengthens the message.

Within the Company the security unit covers all aspects of security, and reports direct to the Company Secretary who is also a Board member.

The Director of Security is sometimes concerned with different security areas such as investigation and detection, national security, commercial security and estate security. The Director of Security manages by means of a coordinating committee drawn from all Company business divisions (see Figure 1).

Each business division has on its board a member, part of whose responsibility and job description is for security within that business division. Reporting directly to that board member within that business division is a Security Coordinator, who has suitable people and resources to carry out cost effective security within that business division area.

There is naturally a variation across business divisions depending on the activities which they are indulging in; for example there is a greater emphasis on computer security within our Information Technology divisions, and on network security within the Worldwide Networks division.

The Investigation unit carries out detective work to help combat crimes committed against the company.

The Commercial Security unit divides between three effective units:

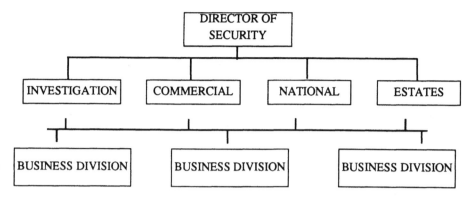

Figure 1.1 Structure of security

- the first sets the policy in the areas of electronic systems, information, and physical security throughout the whole of the Company;

- the second is concerned with checking by means of compliance and review work so that new threats or risks are fed back to be considered in new policies; and

- the third is concerned with running a major programme. This is where the cost of security failures in significant areas is identified and acceptable security is built into business processes and systems. A single programme coordinating the business process owners, security experts and representatives from all those affected by the security failure.

The Estates Security unit is responsible for the physical guarding, including security guards.

1.4 POLICY SETTING AND AWARENESS

1.4.1 Company policy

An important method of getting security commitment is for the senior managers to make a formal statement of their beliefs. The Company has a security policy statement:

1.4.1.1 Policy
The Board attaches particular importance to the protection of its people, information, business processes, systems and property. The Company's policy on security is to ensure that we properly safeguard all our assets, having regard to legal and regulatory requirements, the needs of our customers, our commercial interests and sound business practices. In doing so we will provide a quality security environment for our customers and our people.

1.4.1.2 Scope

This policy applies to all aspects of Company's operations including networks and switching systems, products and services, administration procedures and systems, security of buildings and the workplace, and all internal communications.

Security issues must be considered at all stages in the life cycle of business processes, products and services; from feasibility study through development to operational use and withdrawal from service. It applies regardless of whether a product or process is developed or acquired from an external supplier, and to operations at all locations, including customer premises and international operations.

1.4.1.3 Responsibilities

People are personally responsible and accountable for the security of their operations. Senior Divisional Management, through their Security Coordinators, will be responsible and accountable for the provision of divisional security management and support services using a team of suitably qualified and trained people.

To help everyone carry out these responsibilities, the Director of Security and Investigation will issue appropriate supporting policy and advice, provide certain specialist security services, and is the Company authority for policy on security and will monitor compliance with it.

1.4.2 Baseline policies

Baseline policies have been set within three key documents that are compulsory throughout the Company. These are the:

- Commercial Security Manual, covering security policies for all electronic systems;
- Information Security Code, covering the secure handling of all information;
- Physical Security Handbook, covering policy in the physical and environmental protection of buildings and business processes.

These policies are the baseline policies that apply throughout the Company (see Figure 2). Each business division interprets and adds to the policies for their own particular business area. Security Coordinators are responsible for these activities, and in many cases have amplified and set more stringent requirements, in their own particular areas.

In addition, for security critical items such as products, computer systems, platforms and so on, security standards are produced.

```
┌─────────────────────────────────────┐
│GROUP POLICY                         │
│Information Security                  │
│Electronic Security                   │
│Physical, Building Security           │
├─────────────────────────────────────┤
│DIVISIONAL STANDARDS                 │
│Divisional Policy                     │
│Individual System Policies            │
├─────────────────────────────────────┤
│SUPPORTING STANDARDS                 │
│Development methodology               │
│Secure platforms, products            │
│Operating System (e.g. UNIX, VMS)    │
│Security Architectures                │
└─────────────────────────────────────┘
```

Figure 1.2 Policy hierarchy

1.4.3 Policy compliance checking and other activities

The Commercial Security Compliance and Review unit checks key business processes for their conformance to existing policy. The unit draws members from throughout Company, so individual experts in particular areas can contribute to the right part of a security review. This is important as in many technical areas it is not possible for security people to be fully informed about the risks of, say, a particular operating system.

A security review is not the same as an audit within our Company; the team works closely with the client to make sure that their recommendations are technically feasible and cost effective. A full quality review of the documentation is always held with the client at the end, and this ensures that recommendations are understood and discussed.

As a result of reviews and the making of policies, it often becomes necessary to ensure that suitable products and systems exist to support the security features that are developed. Our Research Department makes, designs, and defines security products, algorithms and systems. This expertise is used to ensure that products are suitable for the threats against which they will be used as countermeasures.

1.5 CONCLUSION

Over the last six years, the Company has developed its security structure to meet the changing business need. We believe that we now have the right structure to meet the threats that we now face. Naturally, continuous improvement is the key, with the costs and assessment of the threats we face being constantly reviewed, and an apt business decision made to ensure that we use sufficient resources to contain the losses that we sustain.

ACKNOWLEDGEMENTS

Acknowledgement is due to the Director of Security and Investigation for permission to publish this paper.

2 Information Technology Security Evaluation: Management Summary

Eric Roche
DTI

2.1 THE NEED FOR SECURITY

The effective use of Information Technology (IT) is essential for increasing business prosperity; dependence on IT is increasing, as is the diversity of usage within all sectors of commerce and industry. However, there are potential risks associated with the use of IT. So it is important that security is considered, preferably from the outset, and appropriate safeguards deployed. The consequences of not doing so can be dramatic, including loss of assets or reputation, inability to meet legal or market requirements, or even business failure.

2.2 PROVIDING FOR IT SECURITY

Security in this context is considered to encompass:

  a) confidentiality – prevention of the unauthorised disclosure of information;

  b) integrity – prevention of the unauthorised modification of information;

  c) availability – prevention of the unauthorised withholding of information or resources.

A significant contribution to the security of an IT system can often be achieved through non-technical measures, such as organisational and administrative controls. However, there is a growing tendency (and need) to use additional technical IT security measures. For example, there may be stringent security requirements before users may access an IT system. For some IT systems, technical security measures will be especially appropriate, for example, where information is frequently in transit via public and/or private telecommunications lines. In such cases non-technical security measures will often not be possible at a realistic cost, or at all.

Users have found it is often cost-effective to use off-the-shelf solutions to meet their general IT requirements, and so minimise or eliminate in-house development. This can be as true for security as for any other requirement. The market for products with appropriate security features has, in consequence, grown. It has also rapidly become an international market, as vendors increasingly export their products.

2.3 ASSURANCE OF IT SECURITY

In IT security, assurance is a measure of the confidence that the security of a system does in practice enforce a previously defined security policy (which defines the security objectives of the system). From a security point of view, assurance provides a measure of the fitness for purpose of the system security.

IT products are normally intended for use by more than one customer. Those developing them are unable to know in advance what assets their products will be protecting, or the actual threats to which those assets may be exposed. In practice, it must be the responsibility of the *user's* system designer to decide on the (security) fitness for purpose of those products, and thereby the (security) fitness for purpose of the resulting IT system which incorporates those products.

IT systems are normally used within a known operational environment for particular functions. Only the system *user* can decide if the security of his system is fit for purpose.

In either case (product within a system; system in an operational environment), ultimately it is those with overall responsibility for the enterprise who must decide upon the adequacy of measures to be taken to protect their assets, including IT systems and the information they store or the services they provide.

Parts of the process of obtaining security assurance may be delegated to specialists either within the company (e.g. DP manager; internal auditors), or hired for the purpose (e.g. consultants; external auditors). However, it is ultimately the responsibility of senior management to assure *themselves* that the security of their IT system is fit for purpose before authorising its operational use.

The processes by which security assurance (confidence in fitness for purpose of system security) is delivered are collectively termed 'security accreditation', and the person who performs this function is termed the accreditor. There may be many other aspects to the *full* accreditation of a system as fit for purpose in the widest sense (e.g. performance; compliance with legal requirements etc.), but here we concentrate only on the security aspects, namely upon security accreditation.

2.4 SECURITY ACCREDITATION OF IT SYSTEMS

Security accreditation of a system can be very wide ranging, going beyond consideration of technical security features within an IT system and, in principle, can cover the security of the whole system, its environment and its modes of use. This may include: confirmation of management responsibilities; adequacy of security policy objectives; compliance with relevant legal/regulatory requirements; adequacy of physical security; adequacy of personnel security; adequacy of procedural controls; assessments of assumed threats; adequacy of technical security features.

An independent evaluation may often be needed to assess technical security features used within a system, due to the specialised techniques involved in such an evaluation. Until recently there was no standardised, independent and general means by which an enterprise might determine this measure of confidence. Organisations may rely on the reputation of the supplier, or perform tests themselves. Or they may prefer to rely on the results of an independent and impartial evaluation against recognised, published criteria.

Such an evaluation will determine, to the required level of confidence, whether the security features are properly implemented, do not expose the system to unexpected risks, and are effective as countermeasures to the identified threats. If successful, a certification body will normally certify the results of the evaluation, confirming that the features evaluated have achieved the stated level of assurance.

In the case of a system made up of several components each of which has been evaluated, there may be several assurance certificates. Depending on the nature of the features provided by each component, some may need a higher assurance level than others. Whatever the case, the assurance certificate (or certificates) provides confirmation to the accreditor that those technical features evaluated are 'fit for purpose'.

A certificate may thus be regarded as an input to the accreditation process. Evaluation, Certification and Accreditation form a hierarchy in the process of assuring that the total approach to security in a system is fit for purpose:

• Evaluation   an assessment of the technical features of an IT system against defined security criteria.

• Certification   a confirmation that the security evaluation criteria have been correctly applied and that the conclusions of the evaluation are supported by the evidence.

• Accreditation   a confirmation that the IT system as a whole is fit for the purpose for which it is intended.

The rest of this document focuses on evaluation and certification of the technical security features as an input to the accreditation process, and in particular on the criteria used for evaluation.

2.5 EVALUATION

Evaluation can itself be viewed as the combination of several components: criteria, methods and Scheme.

2.5.1 Criteria

Evaluation criteria provide an essential 'check list' of what is to be done or tested in an evaluation of the technical security measures in an IT product or system.

The Information Technology Security Evaluation Criteria (ITSEC) have been produced through collaboration between the UK, France, Germany and the Netherlands; it is a harmonisation of the criteria previously produced in each of the participating countries. The ITSEC is now the preferred criteria for use within these four countries and the remainder of the European Community. Its development is described in Section 7 below.

The ITSEC is applicable to both systems and products, and to all market sectors, including government, industry and commerce. Within the ITSEC, the term Target of Evaluation (TOE) is used to refer to a particular IT system or product which is the subject of security evaluation. There must be a precise specification of the contribution to security which the TOE is intended to provide; this is called the Security Target.

In order to cover the wide field of applicability intended, the Criteria separate the specification of the security functionality of the TOE from the assessment of the assurance – or confidence – that can be held in that functionality. Similarly, the assurance criteria distinguish between the confidence that can be held in the correctness of the implementation of those security functions and the confidence in their effectiveness in operational use (as counters to the actual or assumed threats to security that may exist in the context of a TOE and its operational environment).

The ITSEC defines seven evaluation levels in respect of the correctness of a TOE. These represent increasing levels of confidence that can be held in the IT system or product to achieve its security objectives. The level E0 represents inadequate assurance, E1 is an entry level below which no useful assurance can be achieved, and E6 represents the current state of the art. The assessment of the effectiveness aspect of assurance is not performed separately; rather, this is performed in conjunction with the correctness assessment, and uses the results and documents provided for that assessment.

2.5.2 Methodology

In order to apply the criteria it is necessary to have a collection of methods, or a methodology. This provides instructions on how the evaluation tests are to be done.

The procedures and methods of evaluation are the subject of the IT Security Evaluation Manual (ITSEM). An important objective of the ITSEM is to present an objective procedure for the application of the Criteria, so that the independent tests performed by evaluators are designed to meet international standards of objective testing (in particular, the European Standard EN45001 for the operation of testing laboratories), and so that technical equivalence of different evaluators' work can be demonstrated (a necessary technical prerequisite to mutual recognition of certificates).

2.5.3 The Evaluation and Certification Scheme

In order to apply consistently and correctly the methods and criteria it is necessary to have a set of procedural rules or a 'scheme' for controlling the evaluation and certification processes, and in particular to ensure consistent quality control throughout. This operational framework is referred to as the Scheme.

An important long term objective of the Scheme is to achieve international mutual recognition of certificates based upon standardized criteria and methods. For this purpose, each country (in which a Scheme operates) will need to provide the infrastructure necessary to administer, and ensure the quality of, evaluations under its control. The details of the schemes planned by the ITSEC countries may vary somewhat, but a number of principles are common: there will be a certification body which will regulate the input of evaluations into each scheme, certify evaluations, and enter into agreements at the international level for the purposes of mutual recognition of certificates. The stage of development of the national schemes may differ from nation to nation.

2.6 THE DEVELOPMENT OF CRITERIA

Much early work in developing criteria was carried out within the defence sector. The first published criteria, and the precursor to other developments in many respects, is the Trusted Computer System Evaluation Criteria (TCSEC), or 'Orange Book', published by the US Department of Defence in 1983. TCSEC evaluations are performed by the US National Computer Security Centre (NCSC), and this service is available only to US *owned* companies. The TCSEC is primarily concerned with preserving data confidentiality, and seeks to prescribe the functionality that should be built into products, as well as the assurance requirement that these functions are properly implemented.

Consequently, the TCSEC is not readily applicable to all market sectors; in particular it does not address important commercial IT security objectives such as integrity and availability.

As a result, within Europe there have been a number of national initiatives in the development of security evaluation criteria, some of which have resulted in publicly available documents, such as the UK Department of Trade and Industry 'Green Books', the UK Communications-Electronics Security Group (CESG) Memorandum Number 3 on UK System Confidence Levels, and the IT-Security Criteria produced by BSI, the German Information Security Agency. The French and Dutch security agencies have also undertaken work on evaluation criteria which has not been published.

2.7 THE NEED FOR HARMONISATION

With all these similar, but distinct, criteria under development there was a danger that artificial trade barriers would spring up between the groups using different criteria. For a vendor to sell a single product to different groups (e.g. different countries or different market sectors), the product would have to be evaluated a number of times (once each for the set of criteria adopted by each group). The net cost of multiple evaluations would be high and vendors would be restricted to particular markets: trade barriers would arise.

Recognising the common interests and principles behind the various criteria initiatives, and in order to provide a stimulus to the development of the market for IT security products by removing the possibilities of trade barriers arising, four European countries (France, Germany, the Netherlands and the UK) have, as noted above, co-operated in the development of a harmonised set of criteria: the ITSEC.

ITSEC V 1.0 was published in May 1990 and underwent widespread international review. Some 6000 copies were distributed to more than twenty countries and the Commission of the European Communities (CEC) sponsored a review conference, in September 1990, which was attended by about 500 experts in the field of information security.

ITSEC V 1.1 took in the many comments made and was issued in January 1991. It provided for a further round of review, including written comments and a final review workshop, organised by the CEC in April 1991.

ITSEC V 1.2 was completed on the basis of this final review, and was published by the European Commission in July 1991, with the approval of the (informal) EC advisory group, SOG-IS (Senior Officials Group – Security of Information Systems), comprising representatives of all twelve Member States.

2.8   THREE STAGES TO MUTUAL RECOGNITION

As noted above, differences in security standards can create trade barriers, both between nations and between market sectors. The aim of the harmonisation work described above is to move towards mutual recognition of the certificates which are issued to summarise the outcome of evaluations and to confirm that they have been properly conducted. The first stage in this approach has been the development of the ITSEC, initially in Europe.

The development of the ITSEC forms the first step in a three phase strategy to achieve mutual recognition, which is based upon the three components of evaluation described in Section 5:

- harmonisation of basic evaluation criteria (what tests are done);

- harmonisation of methods (how the tests are done);

- mutual recognition between Schemes (mutual acceptance of competence to apply the harmonised criteria and methods).

2.8.1 Current status

With publication of ITSEC V 1.2 the first phase is complete. However, to aid the process of further international harmonisation and the development of a harmonised methodology (ITSEM), ITSEC V 1.2 has been adopted for an initial period of two years within evaluation and certification schemes operating within the European Community. The practical experience thus acquired will be used to review and further develop the ITSEC at the end of this period. In addition, considerations arising from further international harmonisation will also be taken into account, including in particular the US and Canadian approaches to evaluation.

The harmonised methodology, ITSEM draft, is scheduled for early Q2 1992.

Both the harmonised criteria and the harmonised methodology are seen as technical pre-requisites to international mutual recognition of certificates.

At the time of writing preliminary work has also begun on the final step to examine mutual recognition between Schemes, and the prospects for success are encouraging.

2.9   DOCUMENTS AVAILABLE

For further information, and for copies of the relevant documentation mentioned in this management summary, please contact:

Commission of the European Communities
Directorate XIII/F
SOG-IS Secretary
Rue de la Loi 200
B-1049 BRUSSELS
Belgium

Tel: +322 236 3516

Department of Trade and Industry
Open Systems, IT Security and Quality Branch 4d
4th Floor, Grey Zone
151 Buckingham Palace Road
London
SW1W 9SS

Tel: +44 71 215 1318

Head of the Certification Body
UK IT Security Evaluation and Certification Scheme
Room 2/0609
Fiddlers Green Lane
Cheltenham
GL52 5AJ

Tel: +44 242 221491 x4577

3 Closing the Evaluation Gap – The CLEF Experience

Andrew Clark and Andrea Cumming
Logica UK Ltd

3.1 INTRODUCTION

The UK CLEF security evaluation scheme has been operating successfully for the past three years. In that time more than twenty products have been certified through the two CLEFs. Logica has been involved in more than half of these evaluations and has advanced the experience base of commercial evaluations throughout this period. In this paper we detail the evaluation process and suggest how designing security systems and products with evaluation in mind can lead to successful, time-efficient and cost-effective certification. Three approaches to the evaluation process are described and each of their merits discussed.

3.2 THE NEED FOR LICENSED SECURITY EVALUATION

There are many 'security' products on the market which offer protection from unauthorised access to (computer) data and/or system resources. These range from products designed to control access to stand-alone personal computers, through security kernels monitoring and auditing activities on a transaction by transaction basis, to secure operating systems.

Until the introduction of the UK's evaluation scheme, however, there was no straightforward way for a user to know that the products on offer really did provide the claimed protection. Conversely, there were no means to allow manufacturers to demonstrate the effectiveness of their security products in a consistent and independently endorsed way. The US Department of Defence had produced a set of evaluation criteria TCSEC to be applied to US defence systems but that had not been extended into the commercial arena..

Under the terms of the UK national scheme, Logica was one of the first organisations licensed to undertake independent computer security evaluation of products and systems on a commercial basis. That scheme has now been extended and harmonised with others from France, Germany and the Netherlands to produce unified criteria for evaluation and accreditation. These criteria are laid down in ITSEC.

Under the scheme, the successful evaluation of a security product or system in general leads to the award of a national certificate. This demonstrates that the product or system has been found to meet appropriate criteria, and that users of the product can have confidence in its performance.

For consistency, the ITSEC term 'Target of Evaluation (TOE) when used throughout the rest of this document refers to the product or system to be evaluated. Individual paragraph references to ITSEC are shown as ITSEC,xx,yy, where xx and yy are the paragraph designators found at the beginning of every paragraph in ITSEC.

3.3 CONFIDENCE LEVELS

Confidence Levels, which measure the degree of assurance achieved in the correctness of the Trusted Functions, are defined by ITSEC as shown below. For cross reference purposes, against each ITSEC level is shown the US DoD TCSEC class in terms of assurance. It should be noted that, in order to achieve US DoD ratings, all the mandatory security functionality defined for the class must be implemented.

ITSEC	US DoD	
Func Class, Eval Level		
E0	D	Unassured
F-C1,E1	C1	Vendor Assured
F-C2,E2	C2	Independently Tested
F-B1,E3	B1	Independently Assured
F-B2,E4	B2	Structurally Sound
F-B3,E5	B3	Rigorous Design
F-B3,E6	A1	Assured Design

The full relationship between ITSEC and TCSEC can be found in ITSEC,1.35-1.42.

The factors which go to make up the Confidence Levels are the methods and tools used for, and the degree of management control exercised over, the following aspects:

- specification of security requirements;
- architectural definition;
- implementation;
- evaluation;
- documentation;
- configuration control.

Thus, for example, at low Confidence Levels, a plain English statement of the security requirements is adequate, whereas for Level E6, a Formal Specification (written in a mathematically based language such as Z or VDM) is required.

The degree of architectural and implementation separation of the security implementing and enforcing functions is also a major determinant of Confidence Levels. In general, TOEs which have not been designed and built with the evaluation criteria in mind from the outset are unlikely to be able to achieve Level E4 or higher.

3.4 THE EVALUATION PROCESS

Evaluation is a highly structured process, and is analogous to system development itself. It requires at least as much insight into the system on the part of the evaluators as on the part of the developers, especially where security-critical aspects are concerned.

Independent of the concurrence of the evaluation process it normally comprises the following main stages:

- Establish Baseline;
- Produce Evaluation Work Programme;
- Product Assessment;
- Penetration Testing;
- Evaluate Development Environment;
- Assess Operational Environment.

Within this broad framework, specific tasks, functions, reports and deliverables are defined in ITSEC. The generic process described in this paper is focused on a 'typical' evaluation at Level E3 which is becoming a frequent target evaluation level for many commercial products targeted at the corporate computer security market.

3.4.1 Establish Baseline

The Baseline is the key to the evaluation. It comprises ITSEC,2.4:

- either -   a System Security Policy;
  - or -   a Product Rationale;
- a specification of the required security enforcing functions;
- a definition of required security mechanisms (optional);
- the claimed rating of the minimum strength of mechanisms;
- the target evaluation level.

The Baseline information effectively defines the Security Target for the evaluation which will be simultaneously evaluated for effectiveness ITSEC,3 and correctness ITSEC,4. The production of this information is the first step in the evaluation process.

Generally the developer as sponsor of the evaluation is responsible for the definition of the Security Target ITSEC,1.11 – the evaluators assess this definition but are not permitted to create it initially.

A key area in checking the Security Target is to ensure that the security claims or requirements are mutually compatible, and that Trusted Functions are identified which implement all of them. The Security Target is investigated in the first deliverable document that the evaluators produce – the assessment of the Security Target.

3.4.1.1 Assessment of the Security Target (AST)
This document is fundamental to the evaluation process, because it is against this document that all evaluation work is performed.

The AST is produced as a result of the examination of the requirements aspects of the Target of Evaluation (TOE), as defined by ITSEC,3.2-3.4.

The evaluators firstly examine the rationale and claims for the TOE to assess their completeness, consistency and suitability for evaluation. They then produce a set of 'Trusted Functions' against which the evaluation can be performed.

Trusted Functions are those functions of the TOE which have to operate correctly in order that the security requirements or claims can be met. Essentially, only Trusted Functions are the subject of the detailed evaluation work. Correct identification of the Trusted Functions is therefore essential to ensuring a comprehensive but efficient evaluation.

The Trusted Functions list a semi-formal specification of the claims, the main aim being to remove any remaining ambiguity and to add detail which, although not necessary in a set of claims, will aid the evaluators in the evaluation process.

Logica's method used to produce these Trusted Functions has been developed over a period of approximately 4 years within the Logica evaluation facilities and formalised in a study for the CESG. It makes use of simple logic constructs, allowing claims to be broken down to a level at which later evaluation work can be clearly defined.

Although a semi-formal approach to the specification of claims is not required by the ITSEC below E4, the approach in the Logica CLEF is to produce claims in this form for all evaluations at level E2 or higher, since it has been found that the structure afforded by this level of formality can help reduce the overall timescales and cost of the evaluation.

In producing the AST, the evaluators also perform an initial assessment of the security claims against the threats to the security of the product, as defined in the product rationale.

Clearly, given the importance of the AST, it must be agreed by the developer and the certifiers before the full evaluation proceeds.

3.4.2 Evaluation Work Programme (EWP)

After agreement of the Baseline, the next step is the development of an Evaluation Work Programme (or EWP) which defines the type and level of work which is to be performed during the evaluation, the anticipated effort requirements for the work, and a justification as to why the identified evaluation work is appropriate for the target evaluation level. The document also defines any constraints which may be placed on the evaluation, such as specific windows in which functional and penetration testing can occur.

This document is produced for the benefit of the certifiers, and under the current scheme rules is not released since it will contain details of the evaluation methodology, which are currently classified.

The aim of the EWP is to flag, at the earliest possible stage, any potential problems, both in the deliverables which are available and in the work which is planned by the evaluators. The EWP must therefore be approved by the certifiers before the evaluation can commence.

3.4.2.1 Deliverables List

The third document produced in the initial stage of the evaluation is the Deliverables List. The aim of this document is to identify the deliverables which will be required from the developers during the main evaluation. During the production of this document, therefore, any deficiencies in the available deliverables which may prevent certification to the desired level will be highlighted.

3.4.3 Product assessment

The majority of the subsequent evaluation effort is spent assessing the development of the TOE. This is based largely around ITSEC,E3.5-E3.13 for level E3. This involves a detailed examination of the architectural and detailed design documents and the functional tests performed by the development team. In the first instance, each representation provided by the developers and the associated supporting documentation are examined for content and presentation, using the following basic activities:

3.4.3.1 Identify the Trusted Region

In each representation, the identification and justification of the security relevant components and the mechanisms which provide isolation are examined. The evaluators identify the realisation of each Trusted Function in the representation, and then identify 'fences', the isolation mechanisms which will be used to categorise work during the evaluation. In general, it is hoped that these fences will be identical to the isolation mechanisms defined in the documentation.

3.4.3.2 Examine the Trusted Functions

The evaluators then perform validation and verification of the Trusted Functions. Verification is cross-checked to both the preceding representation and to the AST. The techniques used are highly dependent on the documentation provided by the development team, but normally include:

- compliance analysis on design representations;
- source code analysis;
- examination of developers functional tests and rationale;
- functional testing;
- search for side-effects.

The aim of the search for side-effects is to identify any ways in which functions falling inside one of the fences can interfere with, and hence subvert, the Trusted Functions within that fence.

3.4.3.3 Examine fence penetrability

This activity concentrates on the isolation or 'fence' mechanisms which have been identified. The evaluators aim to achieve the required level of confidence that all such isolation mechanisms function correctly, and that no bypassing, corruption or substitution of the Trusted Functions is possible.

This aspect of the evaluation is of particular importance, since the results of this examination can have a significant effect on the level of work which is required during future re-evaluations of the product.

3.4.3.4 Assess effectiveness

The remaining area which is considered (for an E3 evaluation) is the effectiveness of the TOE in countering the threats identified in the product rationale.

Much of the effectiveness work will already have been performed as part of the evaluation for correctness. The results must therefore be assessed in the light of the effectiveness requirements. The following main areas are considered.

3.4.3.4.1 Suitability analysis

The suitability of the claimed functionality against the perceived threats to the TOE will have been assessed during production of the AST. However, these results need to be reassessed if any changes to the original claims have been suggested as a result of the evaluation.

3.4.3.4.2 Binding of functionality assessment

It is an ITSEC requirement that the functionality is assessed to ensure that all the functions provided by the TOE work together to provide an integrated and effective product.

Essentially the requirement specifies that the functions, as well as working correctly in isolation, should not be able to be subverted by other functions, trusted or otherwise, within the TOE. This requirement is assessed as part of the Search for Side-Effects and Examination of Fence Penetrability. The aim of this part of the assessment, therefore, is to draw together any results obtained during those activities and to assess the binding analysis performed by the developers on the TOE.

3.4.3.4.3 Strength of mechanisms assessment

A range of mechanisms ITSEC,2.23-2.24 will be claimed for the TOE, and may include mechanisms providing both confidentiality and availability. The evaluators assess the basis for the claimed strength of mechanisms by examining the strength of mechanisms analysis produced by the development team.

3.4.3.4.4 Vulnerability assessment

During the evaluation, a number of vulnerabilities may have been identified, that is weaknesses in the TOE which allow the claimed security features to be subverted. The development team may also have identified vulnerabilities which have been assessed and for which counter measures are considered sufficient.

The evaluators assess all such vulnerabilities and any possible counter measures to determine whether the flaw can be exploited, and to what effect. The result of any such assessment acts as guidance to the certifiers who recommend what actions, if any, should be taken to correct the vulnerabilities.

Where the identified counter measures are considered to be sufficient, no action will be required before certification.

3.4.3.4.5 Ease of use analysis

The final assessment required for effectiveness is an assessment for ease of use.

The requirement does not imply that the product in itself should be easy to use. The main concern is that the product can easily be configured in a secure manner, and that any insecure configurations should be clearly defined. The assessment, therefore, largely consists of examination of the product documentation and configuration by the evaluation team during the early stages of functional and penetration testing. Any ease of use analysis performed by the development team will be taken into consideration.

3.4.4 Penetration testing

The culmination of the TOE assessment is the penetration testing phase. This is effectively a structured attack on the TOE, based on the knowledge gained during the assessment. The aim of penetration testing is to:

- confirm any vulnerabilities identified during the product assessment;
- attack any areas of the TOE which were identified as potentially weak during the product assessment;
- assess the impact of any vulnerabilities identified above.

As a result of penetration testing, the evaluators will be in a position, not only to identify any faults in the implementation of the security features, but also to provide advice to the certifiers on the implications of the faults, and the appropriate action which should be taken. Thus it may be that certain vulnerabilities in the TOE, although technically breaches of the claims, may be acceptable provided that changes are made to, for example, the claims or the documentation for the product.

3.4.5 Evaluate development environment

The aim of the development environment assessment is to examine the controls placed on the development of the TOE. This encapsulates ITSEC,E3.14-E3.23. Of particular importance is the configuration control system. The evaluators need to be confident that, for example, the TOE evaluated will be identical to that distributed to clients.

More importantly, since re-evaluation may be a significant consideration, the evaluators need to be confident that future changes to the TOE and its associated environment are strictly controlled, and can hence be relied upon when the changed TOE is submitted for future re-evaluation.

The evaluation of the development environment typically addresses the following elements:

- development methodology;
- development tools;
- configuration management;
- development controls;
  - project management,
  - quality assurance,
  - technical assurance,
- documentation;
- trusted distribution.

In order to carry out the work, the evaluators require:

- development standards documentation;
- access to the development environment.

3.4.6 Assess operational environment

As well as examining the way in which the TOE was developed, it is also necessary to consider the environment in which it will be used. For a true product it is impossible to restrict use to a particular operational environment. The documentation is therefore examined to assess the sufficiency of the guidance to the user on the configuration and use of the product.

The aim of this assessment is to assess the operational environment for the TOE, as required by ITSEC,E3.24-E3.37. This is based both on any assumptions which were made in the Security Target regarding operational environment and configuration and on an assessment of the user and administrator documentation.

The evaluators are seeking to confirm that secure and insecure configurations of the TOE are clearly identifiable in the documentation. Further, if any minor faults are identified in the TOE, an assessment is made as to whether the advice provided in the manuals does or could limit the vulnerability caused by the fault.

Finally, the evaluators assess the methods of distribution for the TOE.

3.5 EVALUATION RESULTS AND TECHNICAL REPORTS (ETRS)

A number of Evaluation Technical Reports are produced by the evaluators during the evaluation. These ETRs are documents which provide detailed accounts of every aspect of the analysis performed during the evaluation.

These reports are the basis against which certification is performed and it is important that the level of detail provided by these reports is extremely fine. Additionally the reports will be used as the basis for any future re-evaluation work, and hence must provide a new evaluator with a full picture of what was performed in the initial evaluation.

Currently these reports are seen only by the certifier. However, once evaluation is complete, it has generally been possible to gain the agreement of the Certification Body for release of these reports to the developer.

At the end of the evaluation, a summary report is produced, which generally forms the basis of the certificate.

3.5.1 Security Fault Notification

The Security Fault Notification (SFN) is a report which provides information on any fault which allows a breach of the security claims, and hence, in theory, prevents certification. These are sent to the Certification Body, who would normally then release them to the sponsor of the evaluation. Although SFNs are technically breaches of the claims, they do not always require resolution before certification; on the basis of the vulnerability assessment, the certifier may agree that the flaw can be compensated for by a modification to the claims or by a change to the product documentation. Each SFN is assessed on an individual basis by the certifier, taking into account recommendations made by the evaluators on the severity of the flaw.

3.5.2 Evaluation Observation Report (EOR)

The Evaluation Observation Report (EOR) is the means by which the evaluators can inform the developer of any aspects of the development which, although not causing a fault in the TOE, could become significant at a later date. Subjects covered by EORs could include comments on the development environment, discrepancies in the documentation, or instances of unusual coding practices. EORs do not, unless produced in large numbers, prevent certification of the product.

3.5.3 Evaluation Summary Report

The final report produced is the Evaluation Report (or Evaluation Summary Report). This, as its name suggests, provides a summary of the results of the evaluation, and is produced only if the Certification Body do not agree the release of the Evaluation Technical Reports.

3.6 CERTIFICATION

Certification is performed by the Certification Authority, rather than the evaluators. It is the formal process of the issue of a certificate to confirm that evaluation has been carried out in accordance with approved procedures, that the TOE is free from vulnerabilities, and that target Trusted Function Assurance Levels have been met. The certificate is issued by the Authority, based on the reports submitted by the evaluators.

For HM Government systems, the certificate may be used as a basis for accreditation, which is the process of formal approval for the use of a system to process sensitive information.

A certificate is applicable only to the specific release, configuration, or build of TOE named. Modification of the TOE will, in general, make re-certification necessary.

3.6.1 Certification maintenance

As with any product, certification maintenance is clearly a major concern for the product developer. In order to ensure easy maintenance of the original certificate in a cost-effective manner, it is necessary to invest some effort into the original evaluation.

The quality and level of detail of the documents produced during the initial evaluation will directly affect the scope of the work which will need to be performed during future re-evaluations. The level of detail must be such that an evaluator will be in a position to assess what work was performed during the initial evaluation and how much will need to be repeated in order to maintain the certificate.

3.6.1.1 Logica re-evaluation methodology
Based on our experience of operating system evaluations, the Logica CLEF developed a methodology for the re-evaluation of products. This methodology, having proved itself in practice, has now been adopted as part of the UK IT Security Evaluation and Certification Scheme.

The methodology pre-dates, but maps closely onto, the concepts in the ITSEC of 'security enforcing' and 'security relevant'.

3.6.1.1.1 Traceability
During the initial evaluation, for each Trusted Function, the traceability through all system representations, from high-level specification to code, is established. The evaluators seek to 'isolate' the trusted code, and to ensure that it cannot be made to malfunction by other software within the system. In essence, the product evaluation is a detailed analysis of the correctness of the implementation of the Trusted Functions, and may employ both analytical and testing methods.

3.6.1.1.2 Source code/hardware categorisation
During the initial evaluation, the evaluators categorise all source code (and hardware elements) for the TOE into one of three categories, RED, AMBER and GREEN. The categorisation (described below for source code) is performed using the following criteria:

RED   Red code is security enforcing code. That is, code which is directly responsible for the implementation of the claims for the TOE.

AMBER   Amber code is code which can described as 'security relevant'. Code falling into this category is one of two classes. The first class is code which performs some low-level function which, although not directly responsible for implementing a security claim, is relied on by security enforcing code to function correctly. An example of this class of code could be a disk controller, which is relied on to read the correct data from a disk. The second class is code which, although not falling into the previous category, is not sufficiently isolated from the security enforcing code to provide confidence that it cannot interfere with the security functions. Effectively this is code which does not fall into the first class or into the GREEN category, but which falls inside the isolation mechanism (fence) identified during the evaluation.

GREEN   Green code is code which falls outside the identified fence mechanisms, and hence can be assumed to be unable to interfere with the security enforcing code to the appropriate level of confidence.

Having categorised the code, it is possible for the evaluators, when faced with changes to the TOE, to limit the extent to which the changes need to be re-evaluated. Changes to RED code clearly need to undergo re-evaluation. Changes to AMBER code need to be assessed by the evaluators to some degree to ensure that the code does not now perform some additional, security enforcing functionality, and also that the modifications do not allow any security enforcing functions to be compromised. Modifications to GREEN code do not need to be re-evaluated, since the separation mechanisms of the fence prevent any interference.

By using this approach, it is possible to reduce significantly the cost of any re-evaluations required, whether due to modifications to the TOE to correct flaws found in the initial evaluation, to differences between hardware platforms, or to upgrades in the TOE at a later date.

As is evident from the description above, the application of this methodology requires a significant level of input during the initial evaluation to ensure that the appropriate information is documented. The methodology cannot be applied after an evaluation where this information has not been produced. Therefore, an investment in the initial evaluation is imperative to ensuring the maintainability of the certificate.

3.7 EVALUATION APPROACHES

In the experience to-date of the Logica CLEF, most evaluations have been undertaken in a sequential manner, that is, that the evaluation is undertaken after product development is complete. While this is logistically the simplest approach, there is increasing pressure to couple the evaluation tighter into the development process. In this way the product certification process is potentially quicker and the marketing edge of a certified product is wider.

The three potential evaluation approaches are described below.

3.7.1 Consecutive evaluation

3.7.1.1 Overview
Consecutive evaluation of a product performs the evaluation work after development of the product. This has historically been the main type of evaluation undertaken by developers who have established products and product lines and require the additional benefit of certification.

The work is normally performed in two phases, with some pre-evaluation consultancy provided prior to the start of Phase 1 if required.

Phase 2 then comprises the main TOE evaluation.

3.7.1.2 Pre-evaluation consultancy
Pre-evaluation consultancy allows the developer to gain a clear understanding of the requirements of ITSEC, and the best approach to providing the necessary deliverables to ensure easy maintenance of the certificate across the TOE.

3.7.1.3 Phase 1
Phase 1 is the scoping phase for the project. It ensures that the developer, the evaluators and the Certification Body all have a full understanding of the aims of the evaluation, the claims that are to be evaluated, and any technical issues which are likely to arise.

During Phase 1 the evaluators produce the three core documents:

- Assessment of the Security Target (AST);
- Evaluation Work Programme(EWP);
- Deliverables List.

3.7.1.4 Phase 2
Phase 2 of the evaluation, therefore, comprises the major part of the evaluation effort. The tasks undertaken are those described in Sections 4.3-4.6 of this paper.

3.7.1.5 Advantages and disadvantages
The most significant advantage of this approach is that the evaluation has a clear and stable Target of Evaluation which results in a relatively low-risk evaluation process in terms of unforeseen extra work. The major disadvantage is that the evaluation process consumes time during the initial product release phase and hence the results cannot be integrated with the product definition until some time later.

3.7.2 Concurrent evaluation

3.7.2.1 Overview
Concurrent evaluations are identical to consecutive evaluations except that they

are performed in parallel with the development of the product (or system).

3.7.2.2 Pre-evaluation consultancy

In the same way as with consecutive evaluation, pre-evaluation consultancy allows the developer to gain a clear understanding of the requirements of ITSEC and the best approach to providing the necessary deliverables to ensure easy maintenance of the certificate across the TOE. Because of the parallel nature of the process, however, subsequent work is still undertaken in the two phases, but the interdependencies between the evaluation programme and the development programme demand very efficient, co-ordinated project and programme management.

3.7.2.3 Phase 1

Phase 1 remains the scoping phase for the project. It ensures that the developer, the evaluators and the Certification Body all have a full understanding of the aims of the evaluation, the claims that are to be evaluated, and any technical issues which are likely to arise. The major risk is that the developer produces an incomplete or inaccurate Security Target which results in extra resource requirements.

During Phase 1 the evaluators still produce the three core documents:
- Assessment of the Security Target (AST);
- Evaluation Work Programme(EWP);
- Deliverables List.

3.7.2.4 Phase 2

Phase 2 of the evaluation again comprises the major part of the evaluation effort, although the tight coupling of the evaluation and development may mean that both timescales expand from an ideal case to take into account resource conflicts. The tasks undertaken remain those described in Sections 4.3-4.6 of this paper.

3.7.2.5 Advantages and disadvantages

This approach has the advantage that any potential problems can be identified at an early stage, reducing the likelihood of flaws being introduced to the TOE.

The disadvantage, however, is that problems may be identified during the development cycle which result in modifications being made to the deliverables to the evaluation. Even though these modifications may not be directly related to the security issues of the TOE, the evaluators are required to assess the new documentation, and hence work must be repeated. This makes costing of the evaluation difficult, and such evaluations are normally not performed on a fixed price basis.

3.7.3 Semi-Concurrent evaluation

3.7.3.1 Overview
There is clearly a need to produce a method for evaluation which minimises the likelihood that major problems will be introduced during the development process, whilst allowing the cost of the evaluation to be better managed. It is for this reason that the Logica CLEF is investigating the possibility of Semi-Concurrent evaluations.

The aims of a Semi-Concurrent evaluation are to:

* ensure that the TOE is developed according to a meaningful set of security objectives/claims;
* provide the developer with confidence throughout the development process that the methods and procedures applied are largely compliant with the ITSEC requirements;
* minimise the level of nugatory work which must be performed.

To this end, the work is performed in three phases:
* phase 1 remains the scoping phase of the project;
* phase 2, the intermediate phase, involves monitoring the development process;
* phase 3 is the evaluation proper and builds on the results of the phase 2 work.

3.7.3.2 Phase 1
Phase 1 is performed early in the development process, and is largely identical to the phase 1 performed during concurrent or consecutive evaluations. In addition, however, the evaluators perform an early assessment of the methods and procedures which are to be used during the development process. This involves examining the project and quality plans for the development and assessing the documentation plan.

In addition to the above, this is an ideal opportunity for the evaluators to run seminars or training courses to provide the development teams with a full understanding of the work of the evaluators and the requirements of ITSEC.

3.7.3.3 Phase 2
The aim of phase 2 is then to monitor the development process at a high level. The depth of this monitoring is largely dictated by the degree of feedback required by the developers. The result can be anywhere between a consecutive and a concurrent evaluation. However, the following are the main areas which are examined:

* the development environment is monitored by performing regular visits and interviewing development staff. This provides confidence to the

developer that sufficient procedures are in place;
- the documents produced throughout the evaluation are also monitored. This will in general be an extremely high-level examination to ensure that in terms of content and presentation they meet the requirements of ITSEC. In general, no attempt is made to evaluate these documents at this stage.

3.7.3.4 Phase 3

Phase 3 comprises the main evaluation, similar to the phase 2 performed for other evaluations. However, this builds on the work of the previous phase, which will clearly provide confidence that the documents produced are largely compliant with ITSEC.

3.7.3.5 Advantages and disadvantages

This approach exhibits the great advantage of the consecutive approach – a stable target, together with the timeliness of the Concurrent approach. As a result the developer has a much better understanding of the status of the evaluation during the development phase but without the major risk of resource conflict and rework which is characteristic of the Concurrent approach.

In comparison with the Consecutive approach, the major disadvantage is the increased level of resource commitment needed during the product development phase, together with the tighter control necessary for an integrated development/evaluation process.

3.8 PLANNING FOR CERTIFICATION

As we have suggested, in planning a product development it is important to consider the integration of the product certification into the development cycle. Where a product will have a unique marketing edge, the evaluation process should be as time-efficient as possible so that the product time-to-market should not be unduly delayed.

Developers must not underestimate the level of investment required both in terms of deliverable items and personnel support. In particular, in order to undertake a full product evaluation, the evaluators will typically require access to:

- a target configuration (the TOE itself)
- security manual for the TOE
- design documentation
- source code
- test specifications and results
- support from members of the developer's staff.

In cases where all of these inputs cannot be provided (for example source code in the case of an imported product), it may be possible, with the agreement of the Certification Authority, to undertake an evaluation. However, the highest confidence level which could be achieved in these circumstances may be severely restricted.

One further consequence of not providing the fullest information is that when a change is made the entire evaluation may need to be repeated in order to maintain certification. By providing sufficient input to allow the evaluators to identify the changes clearly, it may well be that only some of the changed areas will need to be re-evaluated, thereby reducing time and effort.

ITSEC provides clear guidance on the responsibilities of both developers (sponsors) and evaluators at all the evaluation levels. Sensible use of pre-evaluation consultancy before undertaking the first-of-type evaluation may well save a developer significant upheaval and consequential costs by clearly highlighting exactly how much support they must provide, both in terms of deliverables and resource availability, before their contribution becomes a critical issue to the evaluation process.

As more products are achieving certification, developers are appreciating that enhancements and additions to their products will mean that re-evaluation may be necessary several times during a single product's lifetime. Certification maintenance is clearly a major concern, and in order to ensure easy maintenance of the original certificate in a cost-effective manner it is prudent to invest some pre-planned maintenance effort into the original evaluation.

3.9 CONCLUSION

The CLEF scheme has been created to support the process of evaluation. Both the CLEF organisations themselves and the staff working within them are individually approved and licensed by the Certification Authority. Only evaluations performed by approved facilities are acceptable to the Certification Authority.

The principal purpose of a CLEF is to evaluate systems and products, using the approved methods and tools defined by the CESG. These evaluation services are available, with CESG approval, to any procurer, installer or vendor of secure systems or products.

Clearly, with the evaluation and computer security experience available within it, a CLEF is uniquely qualified to advise product vendors and system developers on the steps needed to achieve the desired level of assurance. Such specialist consultancy services are also available, provided that no conflict of interest arises between the giving of advice and the evaluation of the product or system in question. A CLEF can also advise on the implication of proposed modifications to a certified product or system.

For organisations intending the procurement or development of secure computer systems, a CLEF can provide valuable advice on security policy and security requirements, including use of secure components, to ensure that the system specification accurately and effectively represents the real requirement. The CLEF can also help in the assessment of tenders, to identify potential weaknesses in proposals which may lead to difficulties or delays in certification of the system.

The three evaluation approaches discussed in this paper highlight the choices available to developers who wish to integrate product evaluation into their development plans. Each approach has its own advantages and disadvantages. To date, the majority of evaluations undertaken have been of the Consecutive type. As the benefits of having a certified security product become better understood there will be a move towards a more elapsed-time-efficient evaluation approach. From our experience, we believe that the logical step is to adopt the Semi-Concurrent approach to gain best advantage of the time efficiency, but minimising the risks inherent in tightly coupled development and evaluation programmes.

REFERENCES

ITSEC Information Technology Security Evaluation Criteria (ITSEC), Provisional Harmonised Criteria, Version 1.2, June 1991, ISBN 92-826-3004-8

TCSEC Department of Defence Trusted Computer System Evaluation Criteria, December 1985, DOD 5200.28-STD, Library No. S225,711

4 Mechanisms of Stealth

Alan Solomon
S & S International

For a virus to be a virus, all it needs to do is copy itself. But to be a successful virus it needs to be as inconspicuous as possible. Like a mouse, its main defence is that you don't know that it's there, because as soon as you spot it you'll swat it.

The generic term for the attempt to remain inconspicuous is 'stealth', but there are various degrees of stealth, and various mechanisms for achieving this. Overall, we have been watching an increasing trend in this direction, for reasons we shall discuss.

Some technical information is given in this article. Be assured that this is not of use to virus authors as it is all published in such standard reference manuals as the MS DOS Encyclopaedia, published by Microsoft Press.

Some viruses are highly visible; for example, the *Burger* viruses overwrite the beginning of the file that they infect, the program no longer functions and the user immediately notices that. There is absolutely no way that you can fail to notice an overwriting virus. We call this negative stealth, level 1. About 10% of viruses have negative stealth, and the obvious question is why? The reason must be that there is a segment of virus authors who really don't care about writing a virus that actually is survivable; all they want is the nice warm feeling that comes with being able to boast that you've written a virus. Boot sector viruses cannot have negative stealth – if they didn't pass on control to the original boot sector, the computer would not boot up at all.

The next level up is really necessary in order for the virus to spread at all. The original program must still run, or substantially so. This is done by adding the virus to the file yet preserving all the necessary information for the program to still run, and for the virus to execute in addition to the original program. About 90% of viruses do this at least. We call this level 0 stealth. But if the virus does no more than this, it will be moderately noticeable for the following reason: people don't look at time stamps.

Just in case they do (many magazines advocate this as an anti-virus measure), most viruses implement level 1, or elementary, stealth.

1. If date and time are not preserved during the infection, an increasing number of programs will have a current time stamp. This might be noticed by an alert user and is certainly visible if you look out for it. It is avoided by using

interrupt 21h, function 57h; there are some viruses that use lower level methods to preserve date and time.

2. If a virus uses DOS writes to add itself to the file and the media is write protected, DOS will give a critical error, 'Abort, Retry, Fail'. This will be noticed – the user may ask why the disk is being written to when all he did was try to run a program. Again, it would need an alert user to spot this, and anyway write protected media don't get used very much. It is fairly easy to avoid this problem; the critical error comes to you via interrupt 24h, and it can be replaced temporarily with a small routine that does nothing at all. Boot sector viruses don't have to do anything about the above issues.

A virus that deals with the two problems above, we would call stealth level 1, or elementary stealth. In addition, in order to qualify for this level, the virus must do nothing flashy to call attention to itself. For example, the *Diamond (V1024)* virus displays every hour, on the hour. A multicoloured diamond pops up on the screen, shatters into diamond fragments, which then dance around the screen, gradually clearing it. If you don't notice that you need new glasses, and if you don't twig that something odd is going on you need a new brain.

At stealth level two, intermediate stealth, it starts getting more interesting. Below that level the virus can be seen with the naked eye, as it were. In the case of a file virus you could see the difference in file size, or in the case of a boot sector virus you would see a peculiar boot sector. It is possible to conceal the increase in file size, and this can be done in a number of ways.

1. The most obvious way, is not to have an increase in file size in the first place. The *Zero-hunt* virus looks for a block of contiguous zeros in the file, and if it finds this overwrites that part of the file with itself. The file, therefore, does not grow at all. When the infected program runs, the virus runs first, and, after going memory resident, it overwrites the memory image of the file with zeros so that the program will run completely normally. The *Rat* uses a similar technique but only works in EXE files where it looks for the block of zeros that many compilers put at the start of the EXE file just after the EXE header.

2. For most people, the only way they inspect file sizes is with a DIR command. DIR uses interrupt 21h, functions 11h and 12h. If the virus intercepts interrupt 21h and traps these functions then it can subtract the virus's length from the value returned and pass this fake value on to any calling program. So DIR looks normal. *Zero-eater* (also called *Zero-bug*) uses this method.

3. There is another way to find out a file's size; interrupt 21h functions 4eh and 4fh. These are the handle equivalents of 11h and 12h, and some of the programs that act as a user shell for DOS use these calls to find out file sizes.

Also, if an anti-virus program is checking on file sizes it probably uses these functions as they are easier on the programmer than 11h and 12h. The virus can trap and fake these calls also.

4. A third way to find out file size is interrupt 21h function 42h subfunction 2. This is 'Seek to end of file' and the file size is returned in the registers. A sneaky anti-virus program might use this call to determine the file size, but there are sneaky viruses that do their subtraction on this also, such as *Tequila*.

Of course, you can avoid such tricks by cold-booting from a known clean DOS diskette, which is what we all tell users to do. We also know that the number of people who actually do this before running their anti-virus software can be counted on the fingers of one hand. We have to assume that people don't do as instructed in the manual because a lot of them didn't read the manual, and a lot of those that did read the manual have decided that it isn't necessary to do what they've been told.

5. One problem with the above three methods is that the virus must be in memory for the stealth to operate, and maybe the virus hasn't been run yet, or maybe the user has cold-booted from a clean DOS diskette. The next way to avoid the apparent growth in file size is to grow the file but not let the directory entry reflect this. The *Number of the Beast* virus is 512 bytes long and replaces the first sector of the file with itself. But it needs that original sector so it stores it after the end of the file, in the space between the end of the file and the end of the cluster. Most hard disks have 2k clusters so about 75% of files will have the necessary space available. A problem with this approach is that when you copy that file onto a floppy disk the cluster size will be 1k at most and high capacity floppies have a cluster size of $^1/_2$k. When you copy an infected file onto floppies the virus will be copied but not all of the original program. *Number of the Beast* has not yet been seen in the wild in Western Europe, let alone in the USA.

6. *V1963* virus (and *V1963B*, also called *Necrophilia*) needs 1963 bytes, so this technique would not be very successful. Instead, it adds one cluster to the FAT chain and uses that to store the first 1963 bytes of the original file. The directory entry is left unchanged so that even if the virus is not in memory the file size does not look suspicious.

7. In the case of boot sector viruses, for the virus to be intermediate stealth it would have to show the original boot sector whenever a request is made to read the boot sector. *Brain* was the first virus that did this. But the fact that it readily puts a volume label on the diskette, '(c) Brain', plus the noticeable 3k in bad sectors on the diskette, really disqualifies it for being intermediate stealth. Most of the so-called 'stealth' viruses in most virus catalogues are

actually intermediate stealth. Very few intermediate stealth viruses are successful, though. Since very few people go looking for viruses, the benefit of intermediate stealth over elementary stealth is not really as great as it would seem. To reap real benefits in invisibility it is necessary to go to advanced stealth. In advanced stealth the virus aims to be invisible to anti-virus programs. But first we shall cover a few assorted stealth tricks.

4.1 ASSORTED STEALTH TECHNIQUES

Certain anti-virus programs work by intercepting the interrupts and blocking 'naughty' attempts, such as the attempt to write to COM or EXE files. If such a program is in memory it is clearly a good idea to disable it before infecting anything. One well known example of such programs has, in some versions, provided a convenient way for users to do this, so that a user wishing to perform some action that would be flagged can do so without getting a false alarm. Some viruses, such as *Eight Tunes*, detect this product by using its own 'Are you there?' call.

Another technique that we see sometimes was prompted by the fact that many scanning programs do a self-check before running, and if there is any change to the file they report this. This would mean that a new virus might be detected in this way. So some of the viruses refrain from infecting such programs; one common way is to look for the letters 'SC' or 'SCAN' at the beginning of, or alternatively anywhere in, the filename. Another string that they avoid is a file with 'TEST' in the name. You might consider renaming your scanner, although it might object to this.

Viruses that stealth the file size often leave an inconsistency between the size according to the directory entry and the number of elements in the FAT chain. When CHKDSK is run it will report these inconsistencies, and CHKDSK is a program that is often run when problems are suspected. In order to avoid the suspicious report by CHKDSK at least one virus checks the name of the program being run, and if it is CHKDSK the file size stealth is disabled.

4.2 ADVANCED STEALTH

A virus that uses advanced stealth is aiming to conceal its existence even from anti-virus software. The best known example of this is *Frodo*, also known as *4096*, *4K* and *IDF*. *Frodo* is much misunderstood. We've seen reports that it disinfects itself when read, which is a rather curious way of describing what it actually does. In fact it traps interrupt 21h, and when any file-related operations are performed it swings into action. When any program uses DOS to read, write, seek or whatever in the file, *Frodo* works out what that DOS call would have seen if *Frodo* had not infected the file and returns that information for DOS to present to the calling program. The result is that with *Frodo* in memory, even if you do a byte-by-byte comparison between an infected file and a clean copy (which would perhaps be on a write-protected floppy disk), the comparison would report no difference. *Frodo* marks files by adding 100 years to the date stamp (hence the alias '100 years'), and even the existence of this is concealed. As a result it is difficult to notice that *Frodo* is present, and tricky to get rid of it.

It has a neat way of concealing itself in memory, too. Most programs that go memory resident and capture an interrupt do so by changing the entry in the interrupt vector table. As a result, some people have guessed that this is the only way to do this. But *Frodo* avoids this method in order to fool programs that check for changes in the IVT. Instead, *Frodo* patches the first five bytes of the interrupt handler with a jump to the *Frodo* code. After the *Frodo* code is run, it then repatches the original DOS kernel back to what it was before, and jumps to it.

Number of the Beast (so called because of the '666' in the code) is exactly 512 bytes long (there are about a dozen versions of it now). It is also an advanced stealth virus, but it does this trick by manipulating the system file tables inside DOS. The 512 bytes of the virus are very tightly coded – it looks like a Swiss watch, although perhaps that should be a Bulgarian watch. If there is any attempt to read the first 512 bytes of an infected file while the virus is in memory, it fetches the original 512 bytes that it has placed after the end of the file and presents those instead. Again, DOS compare and cryptographic checksummers are fooled into thinking that the file is unchanged from the original.

It also has a neat way of hiding in memory. It needs precisely 512 bytes of storage, and it gets this by taking the first DOS buffer and convincing DOS that the second buffer is actually the first. Thus, most memory mappers will not recognise this 512 byte hole in memory, or else think that it is part of DOS.

Amongst boot sector viruses, *Joshi* and *EDV* use advanced stealth techniques. With either of these viruses, if the virus is in memory and you look at the sector that contains the virus code, the virus redirects the read to where it put the sector that it replaced so that anti-virus software sees nothing amiss. *EDV* has some additional tricks. If you look at the place where it parked the sector it replaced, at cylinder 39, head 1 sector 8, the virus returns an unreadable sector error so that you do not see a boot sector in such an unusual place. And when the virus goes memory resident, it first tries to use memory above 640k, if there is Ram up there, so that memory mappers don't see it.

Joshi will survive a Ctl-Alt-Del. Most people think that C-A-D triggers a reboot; actually it is just another keystroke that can be replaced by replacing interrupt 9. This trick of *Joshi's* has allowed it to survive clean-up operations by people who think that all you have to do is reboot and low level format hard disks – not only is this overkill but it doesn't necessarily do the job, unless you do the right things in the right order.

4.3 EVADING SCANNERS

The main enemy of viruses, is the scanner. This is because this is the only tool that many people use (indeed many people seem to believe that it is the only possible tool). So the virus authors have developed ways of concealing the existence of the virus from scanners, or at least making it more difficult to detect them in this way.

Perhaps the first virus that started to do this was *Cascade*. Most of the virus is encrypted using two encryption keys that are variable. The only constant part of the virus is the decrypter/loader, which is a couple of dozen bytes of code that decrypts the rest of the virus so that it can run. This means that the designer of the scanner has only a couple of dozen bytes to choose the search string from, and there is a lovely and obvious sequence to choose, '141$Flu'. In the early days many scanners chose this sequence, but failed to encrypt the search string in the scanner itself. As a result scanners would find this string in each other and give false alarms. These days nearly every scanner encrypts all its search strings to avoid this problem, although there are still a few that don't, or which fail to clear them from memory after running, which leads to memory false alarms. Having only a few dozen bytes clear in *Cascade* aggravates this problem.

The next step was when the virus authors started putting some variable bytes in the middle of the decrypter/loader. These bytes do nothing of significance so can be any valid instruction, but this means that the scanner has to implement wild card searches, which adds some complexity to the program, although not a great deal. *Phoenix, Evil, Proud* and *Virus-101* use this technique. The next step is to make the number of non-significant instructions variable. To do this there needs to be a random number generator in the virus to choose the non-significant instruction and to choose the number of these instructions that will be used. At this point we begin to talk about a code generator in the body of the virus, to generate different randomised decrypter/loaders. The *Simulate* virus uses this technique. It means that, putting on the virus researcher's white hat, we have to implement a search engine that is capable of accepting a wild card that represents a variable number of bytes, although between certain limits. What are these limits? We need to know, because if we have, say, six three-byte search strings and allow these to occur within 64kb of file, the probability of a false alarm is much greater than if we specify that they must all occur within 100 bytes. But until we have disassembled, analysed and understood the virus we cannot make this prediction.

The next step in disguising the virus consists of the realisation that in many code sequences the exact order of the instructions doesn't affect the outcome. For example, if you load the AX register and then the CX register, the upshot is the same as if you load CX and then AX. Putting on the virus author's black hat, if you write the code generator so as to randomise the order of these instructions, it makes it even harder to search for the virus. With the virus researcher's white hat on, either you have to give the search engine a great many search strings, or else you need some way to tell the scanner that within certain limits the order of finding these fragments doesn't matter. Again, you have to disassemble and understand the virus to be able to predict the limits of the code generator. Also, the search engine is more complex again. *Maltese Amoeba* (also known as *Irish*) uses this technique, which is why it is tricky to scan for accurately.

Putting on the black hat again, the next step is to realise that there are many completely different code sequences that accomplish the same end. For example, to copy the CS register into the DS register you can do:

Push CS Pop DS

or

Mov AX,CS Mov DS,AX

and so on. Again, the code generator can implement this. *Tequila* uses this method. Another trick is to realise that many of the registers on the 8088 can be used in place of each other. So, instead of using AX to contain the decryption key, you can use DX, DI or SI for example. Changing the register used changes one of the bytes in the decryption routine. The *Washburn* viruses *1260, V2P1, V2P2, V2P6* and *V2P6Z* use these techniques. In the *1260* virus the longest available search string is two bytes long, there are not many of them and they occur in many different orders. *V2P2* is the same, plus the number of bytes added to the original file is a variable, and in *V2P6* the longest possible search string is one byte long, and there are about half a dozen of these constant bytes which can occur in many different positions and in many different orders. The source codes of these viruses are floating around on the virus exchange BBSes, so anyone who wants to learn the technique can do so. Where the source codes are not available, there are disassemblies that you can download.

Putting on our white hat, how do you scan for such a virus? With great difficulty. Again, you have to disassemble, analyse and understand the code generator that is in the virus, and this might not be as easy as it sounds. But once you've done that, you can determine the relationships between the bytes (rules like, if the byte at offset 14 is a 67 then the byte at offset 19 must be a 73). And finally you can write a subroutine, that can be linked into the software, which can detect the virus in all its instances. But now we are talking about hard-coding the scan as opposed to using search strings, which is more difficult and bug-prone. If you make the smallest mistake, you will either falsely accuse innocent files of harbouring the virus, or else fail to detect one or more instances of the virus, which means that the virus survives the clean-up. Furthermore, if you are using published search strings, forget it – you can't publish a search string for these viruses.

Each virus that uses such a sophisticated decrypter/loader causes an immense amount of work for the scanner vendor, and we are beginning to see some of the vendors give up on these. This, of course, is another encouragement to the virus authors to use such techniques. If Supa-Dupa-Scan (with apologies if there really is such a product) fails to detect any viruses that fall into this category, then any virus author that wants his virus to spread unimpeded only has to use a complex code generator of this kind to ensure that his virus spreads widely. However, many vendors are still staying with the game so far.

So let's raise the stakes some more. Since it is necessary for the virus researcher to disassemble, analyse and understand the virus code generator, the virus authors can make it more difficult for them to do so. This technique is used in *Virus-101*; some of the code is written in a very obscure way and uses features of the 8088 such as segment wraparound. Another technique is to make stepping through the code more difficult; one virus uses the 8088 pipeline so that if you step through the code the computer reboots, but if you run the virus that instruction is a simple jump to the next instruction. That isn't a problem; nor is the technique of disabling the keyboard as you step through the code, leaving you with a dead computer that you have to reboot. The *1260*, and the *V2* series, use another method. Under the first layer of encryption there is a second layer. A few dozen of the bytes in the virus are encrypted with another encryption routine, such that if you simply disassemble after the first decryption the important parts of the virus make no sense. So you have to deal with the second layer of decryption, and you cannot do that by simply stepping through the code with Debug.

The way that Debug (and other debuggers) work is by putting a single-byte interrupt, interrupt 3, 0cch, into the code, saving the byte that used to be there. When the program reaches that point the int 3 is executed, which stops the execution and triggers Debug's display. Another method that Debug uses is to put the processor into single-step mode, and then every instruction that is executed also causes an interrupt 1, which can be programmed to do whatever is required, such as, for example, display the contents of the registers. Debug, therefore, needs to use interrupts 1 and 3. The *1260* and the *V2* series use these interrupts to do the second layer of decryption. Tenbytes does the same, and the Fichv series from France uses interrupt 1 and interrupt 3 with a variable key sequence.

This means that you cannot single step through the virus. Every so often in the *V2* series there is an 0cch instruction in the virus, which calls interrupt 3 and interrupt 1 to decrypt the next two bytes, using one as the key and the other as the byte to decrypt. But you can't write a program to automatically do the decryption because there are also dummy 0cch bytes that don't get executed, so don't decrypt the following bytes. If you write a program to treat each 0cch byte that way you'll scramble those parts of the program as well as decrypting the parts that need decrypting. The virus author has raised the ante; in order to scan for the virus you must understand the code generator, and to do that you have to disassemble the virus, which means that you have to break through the obfuscation. It is all possible, but it all takes time.

When one of our researchers disassembled *Fish6*, he said that it took two weeks to do the virus and another two weeks to uncross his eyes. Disassembling *Whale* is like doing a Listener crossword puzzle. If you ever get cast away on a desert island with a PC and Debug and you get to choose one virus to take with you for entertainment, make it *Whale*. Even a year after it first came out, the majority of scanner products are not able to detect all the faces that it can present to the world; this makes *Whale* quite a good test of companies' R and D in the field. Fortunately, *Whale* is incapable of working in a real environment, but there is always the possibility of *Son of Whale*. The technique of extreme obfuscation is sometimes called 'armouring', but it is a very standard thing in the copy protection field, where the copy protection vendors are keen that would-be pirates should not be able to understand their code. Having discussed the theory of stealth let's look at a real example and the impact of it. The *Tequila* virus is quite common in Europe and it has now just started to appear in the U.S. It was written in Switzerland and a friend of the virus author planted it on the distribution disks of a shareware vendor. This gave it a good start in life.

When you run an infected EXE program it installs itself on the partition sector of the hard disk. To do this it uses another stealth technique called tunnelling. In the case of *Tequila*, it puts the processor into single step mode and calls interrupt 13h to reset the disk. But on every instruction interrupt 1 is called and *Tequila* has reprogrammed that to look at the location in memory that it is being called from. When it finds that it is being called from the firmware it stores that address and switches off the single step. Now *Tequila* knows the address of the hard disk controller firmware and any program that is supposed to be blocking attempts to write to the hard disk via the interrupts is very easily evaded by doing a far call to the firmware. And *Tequila* installs itself on the partition sector.

Next time the computer starts up the partition sector is run, and this happens before any anti-virus software can be run. This installs the virus into memory and *Tequila* then stealths the partition, so that any anti-virus software that examines the partition sees what was there before *Tequila* came along.

Now *Tequila* can start infecting files. It has a complex code generator in the body of the virus so that the decrypter/loader of the rest of the code is very variable. There are a few two-byte strings you can scan for and some one-byte strings that are reliably there. But some scanners have difficulty detecting all instances of the virus and some scanners give false alarms on some innocent files because of the difficulty in doing it right.

The virus adds 2468 bytes to each infected file, but with the virus in memory the growth in file size is concealed from programs that ask DOS for this information, so the virus is quite difficult to see and easily gets copied onto diskettes and passed on.

The main outcome of the virus is a kind of Mandlebrot display in block graphics, three months after installing the virus on the hard disk. The main way that people notice the virus is when some program is incompatible with the virus; Windows is an example of this.

4.4 THE FUTURE

Most of the viruses that we see, are 'noise' viruses; yet another version of *Vienna*, *Burger* or *Jerusalem*. But some of the virus authors are writing viruses that are designed to be difficult to detect, and survival of the fittest will of course ensure that these are the viruses that are most likely to become common in the longer run. When everyone is running the kind of simple scanner that can detect *Jerusalem* and *Stoned*, the only viruses that will spread will be the ones that make good use of stealth techniques. Stealth, therefore, is going to be more and more important in the future.

The consequence of this is that there will be more and more viruses which are difficult to deal with from the point of view of the virus researcher. From the point of view of the user, there will be more and more false alarms as scanners mistake innocent files for some of the results of the sophisticated code generators. Also, there will be an increasing number of situations where the scanner in use is not capable of detecting the virus, not because the scanner has not yet been upgraded to deal with a new virus but because it is simply too much work for the vendor to keep up with the flood of new and difficult viruses.

At this point, we see an interesting cultural difference between Americans and Europeans. Americans are very optimistic about things; everything will be all right, just you wait and see. The epitome of this culture is Superman; if things get really bad, Superman will get us all out of trouble somehow. Americans call this attitude 'can-do' and 'positive'; we call it 'optimistic'.

Europeans have a rather different outlook. Things don't always come out the way you would like; we have seen the opposite too often. We call this attitude 'realistic', Americans call it 'pessimistic'. A famous Englishman (who was half American), near the start of World War II, made a promise to the world in general, and to Englishmen in particular. He said, 'I can promise you blood, toil, sweat and tears'. And that's my promise to you – the blood of the anti-virus companies that fall by the wayside as the problems become more difficult, the toil of the virus researchers as they labour to understand and deal with the stealth viruses, the cold sweat of the users as they realise that they have a virus that their software cannot detect, and the tears that will be shed when it is realised that a virus has not merely erased all the data – far worse, it has made subtle alterations to it over a period of months, it is no longer possible to know which backups are valid and which are corrupted, and it is necessary to re-enter all the work over that period. Churchill also explained something about bulldogs. 'The British Bulldog', he explained, 'has a nose that slopes backwards from its jaws. That is so that once it has got its teeth into you, it can hang grimly on, without having to let go in order to breathe'.

Which explains something else that he said. 'We shall never surrender.'

5 Computer Viruses

Jan Hruska
Sophos Ltd

5.1 VIRUS TYPES

A virus is a purposefully written computer program which consists of two parts: **Self-replicating code** and the **payload**, which produces side-effects (Figure 1). In a typical PC virus, the replicating code may have between 400 and 2000 bytes, while the size of the payload will depend on the side-effects. Typically this is a few hundred bytes.

The side-effects of a virus are limited only by the imagination of the virus author and can range from annoyance to serious vandalism.

5.1.1 Virus types by point of attack

Viruses can be divided into four categories according to the executable item which they infect: **Parasitic viruses, Bootstrap sector viruses, Multi-partite viruses** and **Companion viruses**.

5.1.1.1 Parasitic viruses

Parasitic viruses modify the contents of COM and/or EXE files. They insert themselves at the end or at the beginning of the file, leaving the bulk of the program intact (Figure 1). The initial jump instruction in the program is modified, but program functionality is usually preserved. However there is at least one virus which overwrites the first few hundred bytes of the program, making it unusable.

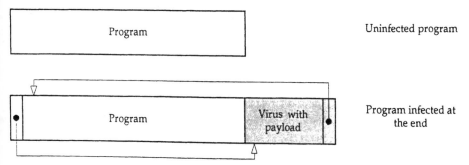

Figure 5.1 Program infection with a parasitic virus

When an infected program runs, the virus code is executed first. The virus then returns control to the original program, which executes normally. The extra execution time due to the virus is normally not perceptible to the user.

Most parasitic viruses, such as *Cascade*, spread when another (uninfected) program is loaded and executed. Such a virus, being memory-resident, first inspects the program for infection already in place. If it is not infected, the virus will infect it. If it is already infected, further infection is not necessary (although some parasitic viruses such as *Jerusalem* do reinfect ad infinitum).

Some viruses do not install themselves in memory, but spread by finding the first uninfected program on disk and infecting it. One such example is the *Vienna* virus.

5.1.1.2 Bootstrap sector viruses

Bootstrap sector viruses modify the contents of either the master bootstrap sector or the DOS bootstrap sector, depending on the virus and type of disk, usually replacing the legitimate contents with their own version (Fig. 2). The original version of the modified sector is normally stored somewhere else on the disk so that on bootstrapping the virus version will be executed first. This normally loads the remainder of the virus code into memory, followed by the execution of the original version of the bootstrap sector. From then on, the virus generally remains memory-resident until the computer is switched off. A bootstrap sector virus is thus able to monitor and interfere with the action of the operating system from the very moment it is loaded into memory.

Examples of bootstrap sector viruses include *Brain* (floppy disk bootstrap sector only), *Italian* (floppy disk and hard disk DOS bootstrap sector) and *New Zealand* (floppy disk DOS bootstrap sector and hard disk master bootstrap sector).

5.1.1.3 Multi-partite viruses

A comparatively recent development has been the emergence of viruses which exhibit the characteristics of both bootstrap sector viruses and parasitic viruses. For example, the virus *Flip* infects executable files (COM and EXE) as well as the bootstrap sector of hard and floppy disks.

5.1.1.4 Companion viruses

Companion viruses exploit the PC-DOS property so that if two programs with the same name exist, the operating system will execute a COM file in preference to an EXE file. A companion virus will create a COM file for every EXE file it 'infects', for example WS.COM for WS.EXE. The COM file will be marked hidden and contain the virus code which will also execute the EXE file. Companion viruses do not replicate widely in practice since the DOS COPY command does not copy hidden files.

5.1.2 Virus behaviour after infection of the PC

5.1.2.1 Memory-resident viruses

Memory-resident viruses install themselves into memory as Terminate and Stay Resident (TSR) processes when an infected program is executed. They will normally intercept one or more interrupts and infect other executables when certain conditions are fulfilled (e.g. when the user attempts to execute an application (*Cascade*) or when the user accesses a drive (*Brain*)). Switching the PC off will clear the virus from memory; warm bootstrapping with Ctrl-Alt-Del may not, as some viruses such as *Yale* survive the warm boot.

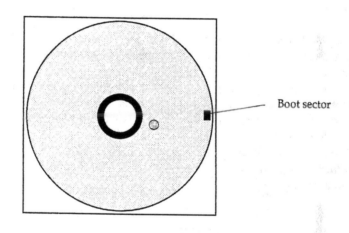

Figure 5.2a Uninfected disk

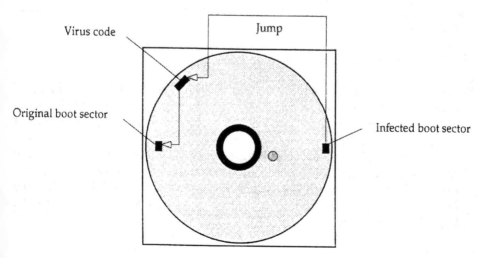

Figure 5.2b Infected disk

5.1.2.2 Non-memory-resident viruses

Non-memory-resident viruses are active only when an infected application is executed. They execute their code completely at that stage and do not remain in memory. Other executables are generally infected by searching the directory structure for an uninfected item (e.g. *Vienna* or *Datacrime*).

The infectiousness of non-memory-resident viruses is just as high as, if not higher than, that of the memory-resident viruses. They are also more difficult to spot since they do not change the interrupt table or the amount of available memory, and their infectious behaviour can be more unpredictable.

5.1.3 Virus side-effects

Virus side-effects (or the virus 'payload') are normally the first things that users notice after being infected. Not surprisingly, they are also the part which is most interesting for the majority of users.

It is normally the easiest part of the virus to program and to **change**. There have been several examples of mutated viruses which had their side-effects completely changed from the original (e.g. *Cascade-format* and *Cascade*).

Virus side-effects range from annoyance (such as the bouncing ball in the *Italian*), data modification (such as the *dBASE* virus) to data destruction (*Datacrime* family). The side-effects are completely open to the imagination of the programmer.

5.2 HOW VIRUSES INFECT

The methods of entry of a virus into the computer are well understood and taking them into account when using a PC is **the first step towards combating the virus threat**.

5.2.1 Infected PC and infected medium

It is very important to distinguish between an *infected PC* and an *infected medium*. The PC becomes infected when virus code is executed, and switching off the PC clears the virus from the PC memory. Most media infected with a virus, however, will carry the virus even after power failure.

For example, if a PC becomes infected with the *Italian* virus from a floppy disk, the hard disk will also become infected. If the power is switched off, the virus will disappear from the PC memory, but **not** from the hard disk. When the power is switched on and the PC bootstrapped (started) from the hard disk, it will again become infected.

5.2.2 Executable path

In order to penetrate a computer, a virus must be given a chance to execute. Since executable objects on a PC are known, **all virus attack points can be listed.** By making sure that the system executes only legitimate, virus-free code, the system will be protected from infection.

In addition to the obvious executable files such as COM and EXE programs, **any file which contains executable code** has to be treated as a potential virus carrier. This includes files with interpreted BASIC commands, spreadsheet macros etc.

On an IBM PC (XT, AT, PS/2 etc.), the following are items at risk from a virus attack:

1. **Disk boot sector and partition boot sector on hard disks** – at least one virus (*New Zealand*) attacks the disk boot sector, while several attack the partition boot sector (e.g. *Italian* and *Mistake*).
2. **Disk boot sector on floppy disks** – several viruses attack the disk boot sector (e.g. *Italian* and *Brain*).
3. **DOS files IO.SYS and MSDOS.SYS** – possible attack points, although to date no viruses infect either file. CONFIG.SYS is a text file and cannot contain a virus, but it could easily load and execute any virus written as a device driver.
4. **Device drivers, SYS files such as ANSI.SYS, RAMDRIVE.SYS** – possible attack points, although to date no known viruses infect them.
5. **COMMAND.COM** – at least one virus (*Lehigh*) targets this file specifically.
6. **AUTOEXEC.BAT** – a possible attack point, though normally affected by Trojan horses rather than viruses.
7. **Applications – EXE and COM files** – several viruses attack these files. Overlay files (normally OVL, OVR, OV1 etc.) have not so far been subject to attack.
8. **Files with macros** – no viruses, other than experimental ones, have been shown to attack these files.

To keep the system free from viruses the user must make sure that the code executed during all of the above steps is virus-free and uncorrupted. Unfortunately, this can be harder than it seems.

5.2.3 Virus carriers

Any medium which can be used for storing executables is a potential carrier of **parasitic** viruses. Any medium which can be used to bootstrap the PC can also be used to carry **bootstrap sector** viruses. **Multi-partite** and **companion** viruses can be carried on any medium which can carry parasitic or bootstrap sector viruses.

The PC becomes infected with a **parasitic** or a **companion** virus when an infected program is executed and it becomes infected with a **bootstrap sector** virus when bootstrapped from an infected medium. **Multi-partite** viruses infect either when the PC is bootstrapped from an infected medium or when an infected program is executed.

5.2.4 Virus infiltration routes and methods

Some user actions have been shown to carry a high risk of becoming infected with viruses. The following list of routes and methods of virus infiltration has been assembled by analysing real-life cases in which organisations and individuals became infected:

- sharing disks between the PC at home and the PC in the office;
- service engineers using the same diagnostic disks on several PCs;
- using pirated software;
- using software from bulletin boards;
- using shareware;
- using public domain software.

5.3 ANTI-VIRUS PROCEDURES

The fight against viruses involves the application of five countermeasures:

- **Preparation**
- **Prevention**
- **Detection**
- **Containment**
- **Recovery**

5.3.1 Preparation

The following subsections outline what should be done **before** a virus attack occurs.

5.3.1.1 Regular and sound backups

Regular and sound backups are especially important in case of an attack by a destructive virus. In case of data loss, the system can be restored as efficiently as possible. As part of the backup procedure, the master disks for all software (including the operating system) should be write-protected and stored in a safe place. This will enable a speedy restoration of any infected executables.

The backups should be **sound**, which means that there is little point in doing them **unless the data can actually be restored**. Backups should be tested from time to time by performing complete restorations of the system.

5.3.1.2 Write-protected system floppy disk

A write-protected **system** floppy disk should be prepared in advance and should contain all system files plus AUTOEXEC.BAT, CONFIG.SYS and any other system files or device drivers such as ANSI.SYS. Note that CONFIG.SYS normally refers to other files which are loaded into memory before the system is started, using statements such as 'DEVICE=filename'. **All these files should be copied onto the floppy disk**, and CONFIG.SYS on the floppy should be modified, if necessary, to ensure that it refers to the files on the floppy disk, rather than the original copies on the hard disk.

After all these files have been copied, **the floppy disk should be write-protected**; this is a hardware protection against the modification of any information on the disk. No virus, or for that matter, any software, can write to a write-protected floppy disk.

If a computer becomes infected, this disk will be used to bootstrap the computer. This will ensure that various items on the computer can be examined through a 'clean' operating system, not giving the virus the chance to employ hiding techniques.

5.3.1.3 Contingency plan

This plan, which will be put into action in case of a virus attack, is usually part of the overall organisational security contingency plan and should include information on the following topics:
- the person within the organisation responsible for dealing with the attack and his deputy;
- the consultant(s) outside the organisation who can (will) be called in to help with the attack;
- exact procedure for isolating infected disks and PCs;
- Public Relations procedure to prevent unauthorised leaks about the attack spreading outside the organisation.

5.3.2 Prevention

Preventing a virus from penetrating an organisation is equivalent to the military physically guarding their camps and states their frontiers. Medical parallels can also be drawn with only sterile surgical instruments allowed in an operating theatre.

The need to communicate introduces a potential virus entry path into any environment. Application software has to be purchased or updated, new operating systems installed, disks interchanged. The higher the volume of inbound traffic, the more opportunity a virus has of entering the environment.

Five practical techniques exist to strengthen the fence: **creating user**

awareness, implementing **hygiene rules**, using **access control**, providing a **'dirty' PC** and providing a **quarantine PC**.

5.3.2.1 Creating user awareness

Creating user awareness is a very important factor in establishing an effective virus prevention policy. Users must be made aware that execution of unauthorised software (such as demonstration disks and games) can lead to virus penetration of the best guarded environment and consequent losses to the organisation.

Strengthening awareness is a matter of commonsense and measures include the use of leaflets, posters, virus demonstrations, presentations, showing training videos etc.

5.3.2.2 Hygiene rules

The observance of **hygiene** is by far the most effective way of preventing a virus attack. A virus program has little chance of reaching a computer if that computer is not networked, has a limited number of users (preferably only one), and is never used with disks from other sources.

The list of rules is straightforward and it essentially boils down to the fact that every executable item which is to run on a computer should be treated with suspicion. This includes **demonstration disks, shareware, public domain** and **bulletin board software**. A simple example set of rules is:

- do not use software 'pulled down' from bulletin boards;
- do not use shareware;
- use only programs from reputable manufacturers.

5.3.2.3 Access control

Access control products can be used very effectively to prevent unauthorised access to computer resources and thereby decrease the likelihood of virus infection. There are two main ways of infecting PCs with a virus: bootstrapping from an infected floppy disk and executing infected software. Infection through these actions can be prevented by allowing only authorised personnel to perform them.

Only the system administrator or trusted personnel should be allowed to install or execute software from floppy disks or bootstrap the system from floppies. Normal users should be confined to using software already installed on the hard disk. A good access control product will allow the enforcement of this requirement.

5.3.2.4 Dirty PC

A dirty PC is a physically isolated machine, not connected to networks, which can be used for playing games and doing anything else which would be dangerous to do on a machine used for day-to-day work.

Employees should be encouraged to use it to try out any software coming from outside, including demo disks and games. No company work should **ever** be done on that machine, and any disks used on the dirty PC should not be used in any other computer. Anti-virus software should be run as often as possible to check this machine for virus presence on the hard disk.

This concept is a very powerful tool against viruses, although it can be difficult to 'sell' to management if budgets and resources are strained. As PC prices are constantly going down, the low cost of a dirty PC (which need not be the latest model and can be second-hand) should be treated as part of an insurance policy against virus attack. Ideally, there should be one dirty PC on every floor.

5.3.2.5 Quarantine PC

Quarantine PC is a stand-alone machine not connected to networks. Apart from having permanently installed anti-virus software, this PC is kept completely clean and is used to check incoming disks for virus presence as well as for trying out new software. It is similar in function to the barrier guard in military barracks.

Only disks and programs which have been cleared are allowed through.

5.3.3 Detection

Should a virus penetrate the initial virus-prevention obstacles placed in its way, there should exist a reliable way of detecting its presence before its side-effects are triggered.

5.3.3.1 'Strange' occurances

Sometimes users will notice 'strange' things happening, such as programs taking longer to load than usual, a disk light flashing when it should not be, program size varying or free memory size decreasing. All these occurrences could be symptoms of a virus attack, but they should not be relied upon for detecting virus presence. They depend too much on the subjective powers of observation of an individual to be usable in a reliable way.

5.3.3.2 Anti-virus software

Various types of anti-virus software are described in section 4. The most important thing to remember about using anti-virus software is that it should always be used on a 'clean' (virus-free) PC. If a virus is active in memory, it can 'fool' the anti-virus program by hiding its presence.

5.3.4 Containment

Once a virus is detected, infected PCs and disks have to be identified and isolated. A contingency plan prepared in advance will be extremely valuable at the moment of virus discovery. Panic invariably results and a point-by-point checklist makes it more difficult to skip an important item.

5.3.4.1 Network access

Depending on where on the network the virus has been discovered, the type of the network and the type of the virus, one may take the decision to disconnect the PCs physically from the network.

5.3.4.2 Disk interchange

Any unauthorised disk interchange between PCs should be temporarily suspended. Masking tape placed over disk drives is a good physical indicator that disk drives should not be used.

5.3.4.3 Write-protect tabs

All floppy disks which are not purposefully intended to be infected, should be protected with write-protect tabs. On $5^1/_4$" disks the application of the write-protect tab means that nothing can be written to that disk. On $3^1/_2$" disks the appearance of a window on the sliding shutter signifies that the disk is write-protected.

Write-protection on disks is a hardware function and no software can persuade the hardware to change its mind and write to the disk.

5.3.5 Recovery

Recovery from a virus attack involves **two main stages**:

- elimination of the virus from the infected PC hard disks and floppy disks; and
- recovery from the effect of any virus side-effects.

5.3.5.1 Elimination of the virus from infected PCs

To eliminate the virus from the infected hard disk, each PC should be switched off and then bootstrapped from a **clean write-protected system floppy disk**. Infected objects (bootstrap sectors, executables) should be identified and replaced with clean copies.

Replacing **infected executables** is relatively easy: delete the old copy using DOS command 'DEL' and 'COPY' the originals from the manufacturers' delivery disks. Using 'DEL' first is not really necessary, but it can help avoid mistakes.

Replacing **infected bootstrap sectors** can be done with tools such as the *Sophos Utilities*, *Norton Utilities* or *PC Tools*, but if you are not absolutely certain what you are doing, 'brute force' approach is preferable. All data files on the hard disk should be backed up first and the disk reformatted. For disks infected with most viruses a high level format is sufficient, while for some viruses (e.g. *New Zealand* and *Joshi*), a low level format should be performed. Data files should then be restored from the backups and the executables restored from the manufacturers' original disks.

Software specifically designed to 'remove' a virus from executable images should not be used (see 4.5 and 4.6, 'Inoculation Software' and 'Virus Removal Software'). This is a risky procedure akin to trying to use tweezers to remove bacteria from an egg infected with salmonella so that the egg can be eaten. It is much better to discard the egg completely and not try the risky approach of removing the bacteria.

To clear infected floppy disks, a pattern-matching program should be run on each floppy in order to discover whether it contains any virus code. After any valuable data has been backed up in a way similar to that outlined for hard disks, infected floppies should be reformatted.

Reinfection often occurs after the 'clean-up' has been completed, sometimes minutes after completion. Although thoroughness will reduce the likelihood of reinfection, one should anticipate this possibility. In the process of eliminating the virus, do not forget to preserve a copy in a safe place, on a clearly marked disk, for detailed analysis. This is best done by one of the organisations involved in virus research.

5.3.5.2 Recovery from virus side-effects

Recovery from virus side-effects depends on the virus. In the case of innocuous viruses such as Cascade, recovery from side-effects is obviously not necessary, while in the case of a virus such as Datacrime, recovery will involve the restoration of a complete hard disk.

The most important thing when recovering from virus side-effects is the existence of **sound backups**. Original executables should be kept on write-protected disks so that any infected programs can be easily replaced by the original clean versions.

Sometimes it is possible to recover data from disks damaged by a virus. This is a rather specialist task best performed by commercial data recovery agencies and is normally expensive.

5.3.5.3 Other points

There are a few other things worth bearing in mind during the recovery from a virus attack:

- discover and close loopholes which caused the virus to enter the organisation;
- inform any possible recipients of the infected disks outside the organisation that they may be affected by the virus; and
- consider the implications to the organisation of the bad publicity.

Virus non-specific	Virus specific
Checksumming software	*Scanning software*
Monitoring software	*Monitoring software*
Integrity shells	*'Inoculation' software*
Virus removal software	*Disinfection software*

Figure 5.3 Types of anti-virus software

5.4 ANTI-VIRUS SOFTWARE

The many anti-virus software packages on the market can be divided into two categories: **Virus-non-specific** and **Virus-specific**. Each category can, in turn, be divided into four sub-categories as shown in Figure 3.

5.4.1 Checksumming software

Checksumming software relies on the calculation of a checksum of any executable on the system followed by periodic recalculations in order to verify that the checksum has not changed. **If a virus attacks an executable, it will have to change at least one bit of the executable**, which will result in a completely different checksum (provided a strong checksumming algorithm is used).

This type of software is reactive rather than proactive, in that a virus attack will be detected **after** it happens. Checksumming software also relies on the fact that the executables are 'clean' (i.e. virus-free) before the initial checksumming is applied. This can be ensured by using virus-specific scanning software to check the system for the presence of any known viruses.

The checksumming approach is the only known method which will detect all viruses, present and future, with absolute certainty. This makes it inherently desirable as a **long-term anti-virus strategy** in any organisation.

The method of performing the checksumming process (the checksumming algorithm) is very important. Three general approaches are possible: Simple checksums, Cyclic Redundancy Checks (CRCs) and Cryptographic checksums. **Cryptographic checksums are the most secure approach.**

5.4.2 Scanning software

A virus-scanning program relies on the knowledge of known virus 'patterns'. When a new virus appears in the wild, it is analysed, and a characteristic pattern of some 16 bytes recorded. The virus-scanning program will scan all executables on a disk, including the operating system and the bootstrap sector(s), and compare their contents with the known virus patterns.

This type of software can only discover viruses that it 'knows' about and as such must continually be updated with new patterns as new viruses appear. This is the main problem with this type of software. Nevertheless, scanning software is especially useful for checking incoming floppy disks for the presence of known viruses.

5.4.3 Monitoring software

Monitoring software packages (also called on-line packages) install themselves as memory-resident TSR (Terminate-Stay-Resident) programs in a manner similar to some PC utilities. They intercept and monitor disk I/O, trying either to monitor system integrity or to detect 'virus activity'.

While this approach is attractive in theory, in practice false alarms can result from legitimate program activity which is misinterpreted by the anti-virus software (this in turn usually leads to users ignoring all warnings!). Conversely, any virus which does not comply with the monitoring program's concept of virus activity will be ignored. The monitoring activity also degrades system performance and can be incompatible with network software, certain application programs and so on.

The greatest drawback of memory-resident products, however, is that **intelligent viruses such as *4K* and *The number of the Beast* can easily bypass or disable them**. The mechanism used by anti-virus software for intercepting disk reads and writes, i.e. to change the vectors in the DOS interrupt table, is exactly that used by most viruses, and can be easily disabled. There are viruses which were designed to bypass specific monitoring software (eg. *8 Tunes* which bypasses *Flushot*).

5.4.4 Integrity shells

The idea behind integrity shells is that a layer is added above the DOS command level so that the shell 'filters through' any request to execute a program. Before executing the program, the anti-virus part of the shell will perform an on-line checksumming of the executable and compare it with a previously precomputed value. If the values do not agree, execution of the program will not commence.

Although the integrity shell concept is very appealing, it is not possible to implement it in a secure way under the MS-DOS operating system. MS-DOS recognises only one type of machine instruction and any program, such as the *4K* or *Whale* viruses, can do anything, including bypassing the shell and rendering its protection useless.

While integrity shells have great potential under operating systems such as OS/2 or Xenix, their use under MS-DOS is not recommended.

5.4.5 'Inoculation' software

'Inoculation' software which labels disks or executables in such a way that a particular virus will not infect them is **not to be trusted**. This software introduces a virus signature into objects it wants to protect, leading the virus to believe that the object is already infected. Apart from the fact that such 'protection' can only be done against one, or at most a few viruses, it is not a long term solution and can introduce a false sense of security as well as false virus alarms when scanning software is run.

5.4.6 Virus removal software

The simplest forms of virus removal software are the DOS DEL and FORMAT commands. The DEL command deletes infected programs and the FORMAT command re-initialises infected disks.

Virus scanning software often provides automatic file deletion and boot sector immobilisation. This enables a quick and automatic removal of infected files and the immobilisation of infected disks.

Once infected items have been removed, they can be replaced with manufacturers' originals.

5.4.7 Disinfection software

Disinfection software attempts to remove viruses from infected disks and infected programs in such a way as to restore the infected item to its previous state. This is not something to be recommended as it is not an easy operation in the majority of cases. Mistakes are possible, if not probable.

It is much more straightforward to replace the infected programs with manufacturers' originals.

5.4.8 Summary of anti-virus software

In summary, the recommended long-term approach is to use **virus non-specific checksumming software, based on cryptographic checksums**. This allows convenient everyday checking of system integrity, secure against any present or future viruses.

In addition, there are situations in which **virus-specific scanning software can be useful**, provided its limitations are clearly understood.

Monitoring software is not recommended as it cannot be made effective against all viruses and can lull the user into a false sense of security. **The same applies to virus-removal** and **'inoculation' software** for similar reasons.

The advantages of the non-memory-resident approach over memory-resident products are considerable. Above all, the operation can be made fully secure through both bootstrapping the computer and running the anti-virus software from a write-protected floppy disk. Furthermore there is no performance degradation or incompatibility with other software in normal operation, and anti-virus checks can be scheduled or integrated into other procedures as required.

6 Security Modelling

John Gordon
Concept Laboratories

6.1 OVERVIEW

We describe a technique, referred to here as *Security Modelling*, which, although it does not set out with the same aims as Risk Analysis, has wide applications in the study of risk, is much simpler to use, and is more general.

The technique is based around a software tool and draws upon ideas from reliability engineering, risk analysis and spreadsheets.

Its main features are:

- it places the user in the active role;
- it enables models of the security features of an organisation to be built and freely experimented upon;
- it automatically uncovers all possible destructive combinations of events implied by the model, including those not foreseen by the user;
- it unifies into a single concept the notions of Asset, Threat, Vulnerability and Countermeasure;
- it enables joint optimisation of cost and effectiveness.

Security modelling relates to risk analysis in much the same way that using a spreadsheet relates to making a business plan.

6.2 BACKGROUND

Risk analysis is a key component of any policy on risk. It enables management to balance security against cost by understanding specific risks to the organisation springing from threats to the availability, integrity and confidentiality of its IT assets.

Risk analytic methodologies are often used for two distinct purposes:

- to understand the actual state of exposure of an organisation with a view to formulating a plan to rectify deficiencies;

- as formal documentation that the risk analysis was carried out in a responsible and traceable manner. This may include the policing of an organisational security policy.

There are some senses in which the second of these roles makes the first harder to satisfy. By analogy, in formulating a business plan one would probably turn to a spreadsheet to gain insight by experimenting with different assumptions about cashflow. But when it comes to proving that the business is properly run one would use an accounting package. It would be hard to design a good software-tool to be optimal for both purposes.

Risk analysis tools tend to be strong in the second area, and there is certainly a need for tools to do this. However, and by contrast, the method in this paper is aimed to be stronger in the first area.

Incidentally this conflict is much less significant with paper-based methodologies which operate through workshop groups, but of course these methods are highly dependent on the attendees and costly in manpower.

The work described here sets out to provide a simpler and more friendly vehicle than a risk analysis tool for actually understanding and experimenting with risk through modelling. It attempts to remove some problems found in certain risk analysis methods implicit in the dual roles, and to introduce useful features found in other disciplines.

It attempts to remove problems in the following areas:

- the user is put in a passive role;
- only disasters foreseen by the participants may be addressed;
- many methodologies are complicated;
- terminology can get in the way, leading to misclassification;
- the method can be rigid and unfriendly;
- relationships are sometimes distorted and imprecise;
- experimentation may not be encouraged;
- there may be no evaluation of residual risk.

The features it attempts to introduce are:

- placing the user in the active role;
- identification of all possible disasters implied by the model;
- extreme simplicity;
- unification of terms to avoid misclassification;
- encouraging experimentation;
- iterative modelling;
- capturing precise relationships;
- joint optimisation of business and security goals;
- residual risk evaluation.

6.3 RISK ANALYSIS

The technique proposed here starts out with somewhat different aims from risk analysis, so we begin by looking at traditional risk analysis and suggest how its dual roles lead to suboptimality. We then introduce the key ideas behind security modelling, and go on to give a brief description of an experimental system and preliminary experience of using it.

Many risk analysis methodologies have been proposed, using a variety of different techniques. These have in common the aims of:

- evaluating the effectiveness of existing computing security measures;
- estimating the cost to the organisation if current defences are inadequate;
- selecting appropriate, cost-effective countermeasures (see [1]).

Methodologies may be qualitative or quantitative, and independently of this may be paper based, or software-tool based.

Paper-based methods are often simpler, more oriented to discussion and worksheets, but more variable and less precise than software-tool methods. Good examples of both are the paper-based method of the European Security Forum [2], and the software-tool based method CRAMM [3]. We begin with software-tool methods.

6.3.1 Passive role

Most software tools for risk analysis gather a lot of information from the user, which later becomes part of the formal documentation. The result is that they cast the participant in the passive role of answering a lot of questions, after which the software-tool makes pronouncements. Some highly respected methodologies, such as CRAMM and RiskPac, contain very extensive libraries of questions, and demand a lot of answers before presenting results.

6.3.2 Residual risk

Some methodologies regard their proper output to be a list of recommendations. This is fine if all the recommendations are adopted. But one would like to know the residual exposure if only a subset of the recommendations is implemented.

6.3.3 Exclusion of countermeasures

Some methodologies do not take account of existing countermeasures. This is usually quite deliberate – the idea being to avoid biasing the recommendations in favour of the status quo. This is laudable, but can be frustrating.

6.3.4 Terminology

The formal terminology can get in the way. For example a second processing centre might be classified as a countermeasure, or simply as a resource. This difference can result in different conclusions. The problem is partly due to the formal need to show that something has been done about the risks, and installing a 'countermeasure' fits the bill.

As another example, some methodologies define the value of an asset (such as a database) as the loss to the organisation if the asset were to be (say) destroyed, which may be enormous. This is fine as a formal method of finding the degree to which the organisation depends on the asset, but a poor way of determining the 'value' of the asset itself. Unless both the data and all backup copies are destroyed then little is really lost. But it is hard to apportion the value between the data and its backups. This 'value' does not obey the basic law of accountancy – that the value of the sum of assets is the sum of their individual values.

6.3.5 ALE

Many methods work by evaluating Annual Loss Expectancy, or ALE. This is the recommendation of the American FIPS-PUB 65 model [4]. Such methods enjoy an appearance of precision which may not be deserved since the underlying statistics may be subjective, may change with time, and are usually quantised in decades. There is danger too that the very benefit of working with an ALE – namely that it is a *summary* – may cause actual *loss of insight* of the contributing factors. An ALE of £1m. might come from a £100 credit-card-swindle occurring 10,000 times a year, or a £1bn. loss occurring about 1/1000th of a time per year.

6.3.6 Paper-based methods

The methodologies which are the most flexible and easy to use are the simpler of the paper-based ones, such as that of the European Security Forum [2]. These methods operate through workshop-group meetings, and by completing worksheets. Since most of the work is done by sensible people working together, the role conflict is much less pronounced than with software-tool methods. The ESF method was developed to be very simple to apply, which it certainly is. It achieves this simplicity:

- by first classifying systems on a coarse scale (A...E) then ignoring the 'less important' ones (usually those involving less cash) at an early stage; and
- by concentrating on 'essentials'.

These methods have their drawbacks too. With such a method only those disasters which can be foreseen by the workshop participants are addressed, and there is the small but real danger of excluding pivotal facts at an early stage, purely on the basis of the amounts of money involved.

Such methods operate by completing worksheets. Being only two-dimensional, such representations can capture only the simplest of relationships. It is common to use different worksheets for Integrity, Availability and Confidentiality, thereby making it difficult to represent interdependencies between these factors (for instance, the confidentiality of a service may depend on the availability of a secure network).

In addition, such a crude representation may not always distinguish whether a dependency is absolute or partial – does the service depend on both A *AND* B or upon A *OR* B? In the language of reliability engineering, the one case is *weakest link* dependency, the other *parallel redundancy*. The one is *fragile*, the other *robust*.

These methods satisfy the formality and accountability role by involving a significant number of senior people.

Having said all this the ESF method has very real strength since it operates through working groups of intelligent, committed people with experience, knowledge, and executive power.

6.4 SECURITY MODELLING

With the foregoing as background, there are three key ideas on which the proposed method of security modelling is based:

- the first is iterative modelling – placing the user in the active role of slowly building up a model of an organisation and adding detail, while drawing steadily more informative conclusions;

- the second is the automatic consideration of every possible disaster scenario, including those not foreseen by the user; and

- the third is the prevention of misclassification errors by unifying the key concepts of Asset, Threat, Vulnerability and Countermeasure into a common terminology.

Some of these ideas are simple extensions of those found in Reliability Engineering, see for instance [5].

6.4.1 Iterative modelling

The idea we are trying to achieve is to bring to the field of risk analysis the same ease and flexibility one has for drawing up a business model.

The idea we want to capture is the way a model may be built up starting from an approximate idea, and gradually adding refinement and precision to arrive at a highly detailed structure with granularity as fine as is deemed appropriate, and in which one can have confidence.

Consider the analogy of how an entrepreneur draws up a business plan. He will do this by building a model of the business, probably using a spreadsheet. Starting with a simple model with just the main headings, using approximations and crude assumptions to avoid extensive research, he quickly gleans simple and approximate results.

The reason for this degree of approximation is to get initial results quickly and to aid understanding. Unless the business is in with a good chance, he is not going to devote time doing a thorough analysis.

If the approximate model shows promise, he goes on progressively to improve it, adding more and more detail. He can build up a very comprehensive and accurate picture. There is hardly an aspect of the business which cannot be represented to whatever precision is appropriate. Because the tool (spreadsheet) is inherently very simple, he feels in control of this process.

Where some key parameter is not known there are several simple things he can do. He can deliberately err on the cautious side; he can generate different models which make different assumptions; he can experiment to find how sensitive the enterprise is to the actual numerical value; and so forth.

If he has any niggling worries, he merely has to try out more experiments. With each experiment the spreadsheet faithfully reports the consequences of each change.

When he is confident that all investigations are complete he uses the spreadsheet to help prepare a report, and he keeps the spreadsheet up to date as a valuable, living model.

As a result of this freedom to experiment, the user builds confidence in the results, since if he had any doubts he would have carried out more experiments.

In short, the tool (in this case a spreadsheet) is used in a large variety of ways, and business people are very familiar with it and naturally turn to it to experiment with ideas, to formulate actual business plans, to analyze existing businesses and so forth. Few would question its utility or its versatility.

We would like to do for data security what a spreadsheet does for business planning.

The idea of iterative modelling is to provide a tool for modelling the security features of an enterprise, starting very simply and adding details as confidence builds, where the user's responsibility is merely to describe the model, and the software tool's responsibility is to feedback inferences.

With this arrangement the user quickly and freely conducts experiments with different ways of arranging the enterprise to keep risks and costs to acceptable levels. Because he is freed from drudgery he is motivated to try lots of ideas and make a very thorough investigation.

Moreover because the tool is very simple, and because he is not presented with a barrage of questions he feels in control of the modelling process, just as he would with a spreadsheet. He is cast in the active rather than the passive role.

6.4.2 Combination of circumstances

There is a folk-theorem which says if something can go wrong, then someday, somehow, it will. Everyone has their favourite story of how some disaster came about from the most innocent set of conditions.

In reality, many disasters do start with seemingly innocuous, but *unforseen* combinations of circumstances which together trigger other events, eventually becoming catastrophic.

It can be quite hard to think of everything that can possibly go wrong. People are better employed at designing models and delegating the task of finding the weaknesses to an automatic process. By analogy it is hard to examine a tyre and guarantee to find the punctures, but there is a simple and automatic methodology which *cannot fail* to find them all – place the tube under water and watch for the bubbles.

So the second key idea we want to incorporate is the automatic uncovering of all possible *destructive combinations of events*. This is what was meant earlier by 'feeding back inferences'. The user should not have to concern himself with thinking through all possible disasters, with the possibility of missing one. He just does what he is good at and describes the organisation he knows. The tool will unerringly find and draw attention to all possible disasters implied in the model, and provide summaries, so that the security implications of the model are brought home.

6.4.3 Unification of terminology

The third key idea is to unify the terminology to prevent misclassification. This is done by introducing a simple unifying concept we call here a *paragon*.

When considering an asset such as a database, what one is really concerned with protecting is (say) the integrity of the database, or maybe its confidentiality, or its availability, or perhaps all three. *From a security standpoint, the true assets are really abstractions, such as 'the integrity of the XYZ database'* .

Also it is quite easy, by turning a threat on its head, to regard an *absence of a threat* as an asset too. Thus 'Absence of fire in the tape-store in the Bradford Processing Centre' is in a very real sense an asset. It too is abstract.

Countermeasures can also be regarded as assets of the same general kind if we express them as the abstract quality they are supposed to confer. For example the 'effectiveness of the Log-On procedure in the XYZ cash-transfer system in keeping out intruders' is another example of an abstract asset.

We use a concept we call a *paragon* to represent any security-related entity which is Abstract, Positive and Specific. It turns out to be easy to transform

Assets, Threats, Vulnerabilities and Countermeasures into paragons, thereby removing any problems which could arise from misclassification.

Returning to the example given earlier of whether to classify a second processing centre as a countermeasure or a resource, the answer is neither, it is just a paragon.

There is something else which can be subsumed into the paragon concept as well. Ultimately all disasters are governed by luck. After all possible precautions have been taken, *all that remains is pure chance*. Disasters are held at bay solely by the good fortune that none of the thousands of statistically possible destructive combinations of events which could happen, actually do not. Since good fortune (such as 'The absence of attempts at hacking into the XYZ database') is Abstract, Positive and Specific, *it too is a paragon*.

Security modelling thereby brings out into the open the very real role played by luck. Luck, like most other things is represented as a paragon.

Finally, the concept of the paragon is so general that it is possible to include business goals along with security targets (represented by paragons of course), thereby jointly minimising cost and effectiveness.

6.4.4 Relationships

The final component which enables us to build models is the *relationship*. The interdependencies between the various entities in an organisation are represented by relationships between paragons. In security modelling, a relationship is somewhat like an algebraic or logical expression. It describes the way that one paragon depends upon others. Relationships can also be expressed graphically, which makes it very easy to visualise them.

There are no restrictions on what dependencies are permitted, and so the most subtle relationships can be captured, including many which are quite impossible by conventional risk analysis methods.

For example, we can if we wish capture as a set of *relationships* between *paragons* ideas such as:

- the confidentiality of a service may depend on the availability of a secure network;

- a user-hostile security procedure may lower staff morale which may affect other things;

- customers may not like certain security procedures and so will use the services less, which will reduce sales.

Paragons may have 'value'; the relationships between them take care of the dependencies. Thus the value of a business need not be concentrated in its databases since the relationships look after the details.

6.5 EXPERIMENTAL SYSTEM

An object-oriented software tool incorporating all these ideas is under development.

In this *Security Modelling Toolkit* (SMT), written in C++, paragons are objects, thereby easing the problems of demonstrating the correctness of the implementation. Each paragon is either dependent or independent, according to whether its characteristics are known, or are the subject of investigation.

Borrowing from reliability engineering, SMT work with reliabilities and MTBFs (see for example [5]).

SMT draws relationships graphically, both on screen and on paper to assist group discussion.

The way SMT works is by determining all the destructive combinations of circumstances implied by the model, and by using simple, graphical tools to illustrate them and to provide summaries. By changing the model it is easy to find the best ways of organising the business to minimise risk for given cost, or security costs for given risk, or maximise overall profit including costs of security, or any other criterion.

It keeps a record of all the experiments so that the user does not need to keep notes, and these records can later be used to help write a report.

6.6 EXPERIENCE

Several surprising and encouraging observations have come out of the experience of using the tool.

6.6.1 Structure is paramount

Firstly the estimated exposure to which an organisation is subject obviously depends on:

- the structure of the organisation; and

- the statistics of incidents which constitute destructive combinations of events.

An observation of profound importance (which will come as no surprise to those experienced in risk analysis), was that of these two, the first dominates to a massive extent. The amount of (say) hacking-induced damage is much more influenced by having a hacking-resistant organisational structure than by variations in the incidence of attempts by hackers. Risk is dominated by Structure.

The corollary is that *errors in estimating* the underlying statistics have a smaller affect on the estimated exposure than changes in organisational structure. Having statistics which may not be 100% precise is no barrier to building a more resilient organisation.

This is exactly what we would like to hear. The statistical data will always be incomplete and approximate. The important lesson is that for large variations in the assumed underlying statistics, the choice of which structure is best is unaffected.

6.6.2 Robustness may not be expensive

The second observation is that by removing the distinction between countermeasures and resources it is often possible to increase the resilience of a system without introducing any formal countermeasures. Since security modelling is about relationships, it is easy to see if merely changing relationships can reduce exposure.

6.6.3 Surprises

Thirdly, it often comes about that surprising and non-intuitive discoveries regarding the exposure of different ways of arranging a business come to light. On careful checking of course, these turn out to be correct, but might not have been anticipated without the tool. When investigating the improvement in resilience given by a backup processing site, the result was disappointing. On examination a single-failure mode was uncovered in the form of a no-strike agreement common to both sites.

We do not wish to make exaggerated claims, since of course the inference about the no-strike agreement could not have happened unless someone put certain data into the model in the first place. Nevertheless it is certainly reassuring to know that a model has been tested for all possible destructive chains of events.

6.6.4 Psychology

The fourth discovery is more psychological than technical. It is the way in which freely carrying out experiments affects one's *belief*, and the spin-off this has on one's behaviour and commitment.

After experimenting in an inhibited way, freely changing both the statistics and the structure of the organisation, one is eventually forced to accept that certain ways of organising a business really are very much better than others, from both cost and effectiveness standpoints.

By contrast, merely answering lots of questions and being told what countermeasure to install, has a lesser effect on belief and hence will not engender a strong commitment to do something about it.

Security modelling seems to offer a number of contributions to improving data security.

REFERENCES

[1] W. Caelli, D. Longley, M. Shain, Information Security for Managers. Stockton Press, 1989.

[2] Business Risk Analysis: Establishing a risk analysis method which is easy to understand and simple to apply. European Security Forum, from Coopers and Lybrand, Europe.

[3] CCTA Risk Analysis and Management Methodology. Crown Copyright.

[4] Guideline for Automatic Data Processing Risk Analysis, Federal Information Processing Standard 65. National Bureau of Standards, August 1979.

[5] Patrick D. T. O'Connor, Practical Reliability Engineering. John Wiley & Sons, 2nd edn., 1981.

7 Secure Delivery of Software

Fiona Williams and Samantha Green
Data Security Group National Physical Laboratory

This paper proposes a solution to the delivery of evaluated software to the customer by applying a checkable digital stamp to it. The stamp will perform two functions; it will enable the customer to ensure the integrity software and its validity. By integrity we mean the prevention of unauthorised amendment or deletion of data, but this does not ensure the source of the software. We use the term validity to mean that the source of the software is genuine, that the piece of software is a particular version and that it was received from an evaluating authority.

7.1 BACKGROUND

Research is currently underway in the area of evaluation methods; of special interest to us are the methods of testing implementations of data security standards. Once these implementations have been evaluated, it is important that the purchaser of this software is confident that the version he has is indeed a valid copy and not some other version.

The idea of stamping evaluated software gives the impression of applying some identifier to it like a physical mark on the disk. This action satisfies the requirement of marking the evaluated software (like the BSI kite mark), but it does not guarantee the integrity of the software once it has been distributed. The evaluated software can still be read, copied, used or altered by an unauthorised party. To ensure the integrity we need to provide a checking facility that the purchaser may use to ascertain that the software has not been changed. This facility would incorporate a reference to the certificate of evaluation, providing validity of the software version. The stamp could not be a physical one (ie on the disk) because we need to ensure the software itself. This would also allow software distributed via a network to be stamped.

The stamp will endeavour to meet the following minimum requirements:-

1. Ensure the validity of the software version and source.
2. Ensure its integrity by enabling any tampering with the software to be detected.

The requirements for stamping can be met without the need for concealing the software. The software is not secret and it will not cause any harm if it is read by a third party, only if it is tampered with.

7.2 PROPERTIES OF A STAMP

Since the requirements of the stamp do not require the software to be concealed, the evaluated software can be sent to the receiver in plaintext. The stamp will be created using a calculation on the evaluated software, and can be appended to the software file. The method chosen to create the stamp must be able to deal with any size of file, and must use the whole of the file.

A simple method would be an approach similar to check-summing. A checksum is an arithmetic or logical combination of all the data in a block, which is used to check the integrity of the block. An algorithm is applied to the software to create the checksum, which is then appended to the evaluated software, and the software distributed. The checksum is checked by the software receiver. This simple precaution could be circumvented if the enemy knew the checksum algorithm because he could recalculate the value following an unauthorised alteration, and append the new checksum to the altered software.

The software we are concerned with in this report is subjected to an evaluation process before being issued with a certificate number. Software should not be stamped until after it has been evaluated because

1. It would be stamping untested software (which is a potential security risk, especially if it was only successfully evaluated software was stamped). The process would also be a waste of time if the software failed the evaluation.

2. The certificate number should be used in the stamping process as a validity check for the purchaser.

If the software is to be copied many times, it would be impractical to consider evaluating and stamping each individually. Therefore the software should be evaluated and stamped, then copied for distribution. The security of the software between evaluation and stamping is very important.

The certificate number allows the software to be referenced to a test report. The number will refer to the implementation type, eg 'MAA via VDM written at NPL version 3'. Each new version would have a different certificate number. The certificate number will be used in the stamping process and will be readable by the purchaser for verification.

The stamp must have the property that it can be re-checked as many times as the receiver requires. For example, the receiver may simply want to check the software once when he first receives it, or he may check it daily, monthly or every time he uses it. The checking process should not require the receiver to communicate back to the stamping authority.

The receiver will also require software to perform the check on the stamped software. This software should be readily available and not have to be secretly issued and controlled by an external body. Similarly, if the checking process uses keys, the key management requirements should be as simple as possible.

7.3 THE STAMPING TECHNIQUE

There are various established cryptographic methods available, but the technique chosen for stamping must satisfy the criteria in the previous section. It can be seen that a hash followed by a digital signature can fulfil this role. A hash function takes as input a message of any length and outputs a fixed length 'hash' which is shorter than the input. The output hash depends on the whole of the input message. The hash must be such that it is computationally infeasible to deduce the original message and that it is also infeasible to create the same hash with another message.

The hash function provides the basis for integrity but is not in its self sufficient as the software could be tampered with and the hash value re-calculated, therefore it is necessary to introduce some way of proving that the message has come from the true stamping authority and remove the ability to re-calculate hash values. This is done subjecting the hash function output to an asymmetric digital signature. Asymmetric cryptography uses two keys; a secret key known to just one party, and a public key known to everyone. The secret key can decipher text enciphered by the public key.

7.4 STAMPING METHODOLOGY

Here we present one possible scheme for stamping of software making use of a hashing algorithm and a digital signature.

The following text refers to Figure 1: Stamping methodology. The stamping authority is the place where the evaluated software will be stamped after evaluation but before copying for distribution. Each stamping authority generates two keys; a public key and secret key. The same key set is used for every piece of software the authority stamps. The secret key is known only to the stamping authority, but the public key is published in a public directory, along with the public keys from other stamping authorities. A trusted public directory can be used to issue keys for many applications; this system assures the receiver of the key that the public key is genuine.

The evaluated software to be stamped has its certificate number appended to the file. The software is passed through the hashing algorithm to produce a short length hash, 'Hash A'. 'Hash A' is signed using the secret key of the stamping authority. The signature is attached to the end of the software file prior to distribution.

When the evaluated software has been stamped, details of the software together with its certificate number and the signature are made available for prospective users. The evaluated software is distributed in plaintext format, enabling the certificate number and signature to be read at the end of the software file. The certificate number allows the receiver to identify the software and serves as a reference for the receiver to obtain the correct public key from the trusted directory. It is pointless for a malicious attack to change the certificate number as this will result in an incorrect check during the verification process.

The receiver now has possession of the software file containing the evaluated software with certificate number and signature appended, and access to the public key via public directories. The receiver passes the evaluated software with certificate number through the hashing algorithm to produce 'Hash B'. Using the public key the signature is unsigned to reveal 'Hash C', and the receiver compares 'Hash B' and 'Hash C'. Any differences in the hashes results in a negative check and the receiver must assume the software corrupt. If 'Hash B' and 'Hash C' are identical the receiver can be satisfied that the software is genuine (ie has not been corrupted since it was generated by the stamping authority whose public key was obtained).

7.5 CONCLUSION

We have presented a technique which will detect the slightest change in a piece of software, and so protect against the unauthorised insertion of hidden functions and other malicious tampering. Clearly stamping is not only relevant to evaluated software, but to any application in which assurance of the integrity and validity of data is important.

We must note here that the stamping scheme proposed relies upon the integrity of any stamp checking software, the secrecy of the secret key and the availability of a trusted directory to manage the public keys. The checking software could be replaced by dummy software which appeared to be performing a check and supplied the relevant success message. Unfortunately we cannot provide the answer by stamping the checking software also!

There are three aspects of stamping which would need to be publicised: firstly that a stamping authority is allowed to stamp evaluated software; details of the available stamped software and corresponding certificate numbers; and details of how to obtain a genuine public key.

The stamping methodology could be used, for example, by the UK Information Technology Security Evaluation and Certification Scheme[1] (the

---

[1] Further information on the Scheme can be obtained from Senior Executive of the Certification Body, UK IT Security Evaluation and Certification Scheme, Room 2/0804, Fiddlers Green Lane, Cheltenham, Gloucestershire. GL52 5AJ. Telephone 0242-221491

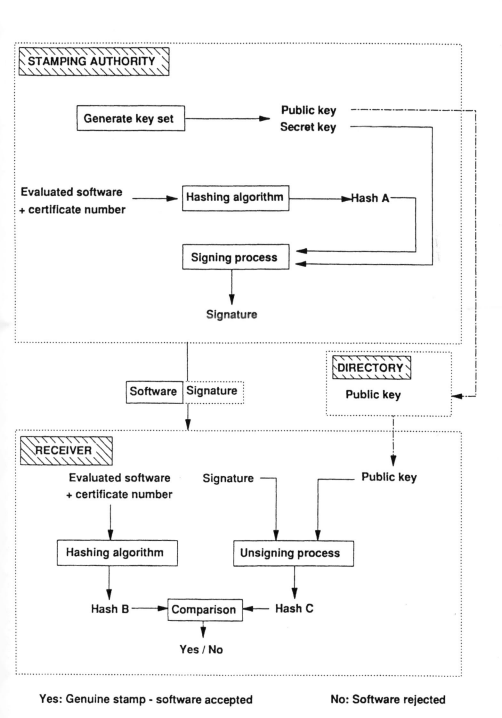

Figure 7.1 Stamping methodology

'Scheme'). The Scheme allows for the provision of independent evaluations of IT products with security features. The evaluations are performed by Commercial Licensed Evaluation Facilities (CLEFs), which are accreditated by the National Measurement Accreditation Service (NAMAS). The evaluations are performed against the Information Technology Security Evaluation Criteria[2] (ITSEC).

One of the aspects of stamping we have not addressed is that of the legal implications. What commitment is the stamping authority making by the act of stamping the software, what are the consequential liabilities? Does the stamp have any legally binding consequences?

ACKNOWLEDGEMENTS

This work forms part of NPL's programme on Data Security which is sponsored by the Information Technology Division of the Department of Trade and Industry.

This paper is based on an NPL report DITC 198/92 Software Stamping[3].

---

[2] ITSEC Provisional Harmonised Criteria published by CEC COM(90)314 June 91.

[3] Copies of all NPL Data Security Group reports may be obtained by writing to the authors.

8 Digital Signatures for Non-Repudiation

Fred Piper
Royal Holloway and Bedford New College (University of London)

8.1 INTRODUCTION

The migration to paperless trading has forced companies to consider various aspects of security which they had previously taken for granted. Traditionally many businesses have placed great reliance on the fact that their employees recognise their colleagues. Great faith is placed in hand-written signatures which we attach to letters, contracts etc. Furthermore we are happy with the concepts of achieving privacy for our communications by such simple means as sealing an envelope or conducting conversations in closed rooms.

In the automated office, face-to-face meetings and hand-written correspondence are replaced by digital electronic communications and it is important that this transition should not introduce extra insecurity. Thus the designers of those communications networks are faced with the challenge of finding effective electronic 'equivalents' for those traditional security measures which rely on personal contact.

In this paper we discuss some of the techniques used to give the recipient of a message confidence in:

- the identity of the originator of a message;
- the fact that the contents of the message have not been altered;
- the fact that the sender will not be able to deny sending the message.

We will, in particular, consider digital signatures and discuss how effective they might be in replacing the traditional hand-written signatures.

8.2 A BRIEF DISCUSSION OF CRYPTOGRAPHY

The following diagram describes a typical cipher system.

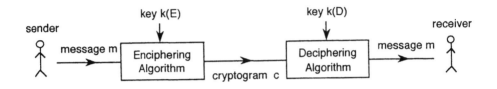

Figure 8.1 A cipher system

From the diagram we can see that there are two cryptographic keys involved, the enciphering key k(E) which is used by the sender and the deciphering key k(D) used by the receiver. The object of the exercise is that any interceptor who obtains c should not be able to deduce the message m even if he knows the deciphering algorithm. Although we do not intend to discuss encryption algorithms in detail, it is important to realise that there are two fundamentally different families of algorithms. In one family, the **conventional** or **symmetric** systems, it is easy to compute k(D) from knowledge of k(E). (A familiar example of this type of algorithm is the Data Encryption Standard (DES) where the two keys are the same.) In the second family, the **asymmetric** or **public key** systems, it is computationally infeasible to deduce k(D) from k(E). (Two familiar examples of this type of algorithm are RSA and El Gamal.)

If we use the terminology associated with physical locks and key then in a symmetric cipher anyone who can 'lock' a message can 'unlock' it but, in a public key system, while anyone can 'lock' a message only the holder of the secret key can 'unlock' it. The analogue with the physical situation is illustrated in Figure 2.

Mortice Lock.
If you can lock it then
you can unlock it.

Bevelled Sprung lock.
Anyone can lock it, only
keyholder can unlock it.

Figure 8.2

While the technical details of specific algorithms are not relevant to this paper, it is important to realise that users of symmetric cipher systems share the same secret knowledge and, therefore, there is some form of trust between them. For users of a public key system the situation is totally different. The sender and receiver have different secret keys and there is no need for trust between them. Indeed there is no need for them to 'know' each other and, in many situations, a user may be quite happy for everybody to know his public key.

8.3 USER AUTHENTICITY AND MESSAGE INTEGRITY

There are many situations where secrecy is not needed and the only security requirement is that the receiver should be confident that the contents of a message have not been altered since it left the sender and that the identity of the sender is not misrepresented. In other words the receiver needs assurances concerning the integrity of the message and the authenticity of its origin. The provision of authentication is one of the principle applications of modern cryptography and it is probably true that this is the most important use of encryption.

One possible solution involves the use of a conventional symmetric key cryptographic algorithm such as DES. In this scenario the sender uses the algorithm with a secret key, known only to the sender and receiver, to produce a 'cryptographic check sum' from the message. This check sum, whose value should depend upon each bit of the message, is then appended to the message prior to transmission. Since this cryptographic check sum for a given message can only be computed by someone who knows the secret key, anyone who alters the message will be unable to make the appropriate change to the cryptographic check sum. Thus the participants can be confident that, so long as they manage to keep the key value secret, no third party can alter their messages without detection. A particular method for computing the cryptographic check sum, which is often called a MAC (Message Authentication Code), is frequently used by financial institutions and is described in ANSI X9.9.

This solution to the message integrity problem is perfectly acceptable provided that the participants have faith in their ability to keep the key value secret and provided there is never a dispute between the sender and receiver. Furthermore, it may also be sufficient to convince the receiver of the sender's identity.

8.4 THE LIMITATIONS OF SYMMETRIC AUTHENTICATION SCHEMES

The fundamental property of the type of authentication scheme described in the last section is that both parties have the same (secret) knowledge and are capable of performing the same calculations. Indeed, when the receiver wants to check the authentication value attached by the sender he performs the same calculation and checks that his answer is the same. Thus the receiver has the capability to alter the message and compute the authentication value for the altered message. If he were to do this and the two parties entered into a dispute about which message was sent then, since both messages will be accompanied by correct authentication values, there will be no way for a third party to arbitrate.

Although there are many situations where this is acceptable there are also situations where it is imperative that the receiver should not be able to impersonate the sender.

8.5 DIGITAL SIGNATURES

The concept of a 'digital signature' was first discussed by Diffie and Hellman in their classic paper 'New Directions in Cryptography' and has since been the subject of numerous research papers, conference lectures etc. In general terms a digital signature should comprise some data which establishes that the signer was the originator. Moreover it must be such that the receiver can save it as evidence which can be presented to a referee who can then check the validity of the signature and settle any dispute. It should thus prevent the following types of fraud:

- the forging of a signature by the receiver (or any third party);
- the repudiation of the transmission of a message by the sender.

8.5.1 Basic properties

If digital signatures are to be as widely used as written signatures and accepted for such important tasks as signing legal contracts then they must have those properties of the written signature which make it such a workable and reliable form of authentication. In particular it must be

- easy to produce;
- easy to recognise;
- difficult to forge.

A digital signature is usually represented as a string of bits. It may be appended to a message or the message may form an integral part of it. Thus, by its very nature, it differs from a written signature. Producing a written signature is a physical process, considered to be intrinsic to the person who is signing. It is this uniqueness which identifies the signer and means that a signer cannot later repudiate his signature. In contrast, a digital signature is produced by machine. Instead of the signer performing a physical process, the signer merely provides some input to the process and it is this input which determines what particular pattern of bits makes up the digital signature. The aim is that no other person should be able to produce the same pattern of bits which, of course, means that they must not know the signer's input. Thus it is the use of the signer's input which identifies him. The signer's input may be some (secret) information that only he knows or a physical characteristic such as a fingerprint. Since it is the use of the signer's input which identifies him, if the input is secret information then the signature only identifies the signer as someone who knows the secret information. It is clearly possible that if someone can obtain that information then they will be able to impersonate the signer.

Another fundamental property of a person's written signature is that it is the same on all documents. Although a difficult task, a forger may, therefore, be able to learn from studying examples of the signature and so duplicate it (without detection). The security of a written signature lies in the difficulty of producing undetectable forgeries. Furthermore, for written signatures, which are physically attached to a paper document, it is the ability to detect whether or not a document has been 'doctored' which guarantees that the document is one that was signed.

It is also, perhaps, worth making the trivial observation that if only the last page of a manuscript is signed then all earlier pages can be altered without detection. Thus if there is a requirement for a multi-page document to be authenticated then each individual page must be signed.

In contrast, since there is no physical way of determining how a digital signal was produced or what input was given and since a digital signal is easily replicated, a digital signature must be different for each message. Moreover it is the particular pattern of bits of each individual digital signature which guarantees which message was signed and so, to prevent the substitution of an (altered) message to correspond to a signature, the signature must be a function which is dependent on all of the message. A forger having seen many examples of a person's digital signature should be no better informed as to how to produce a valid digital signature for another message.

8.5.2 Hashing functions

When a message is too long for the signing process to regard it as a single block which, for the RSA signature schemes, means more than the size of the modulus, typically 512 bits, then there are two possible procedures. The first is to divide the message into blocks of the appropriate size and to sign each individual block. However this tends to be expensive and, if both the message and signed form are sent, produces an unacceptable message extension. The more common procedure is to use a hash function to produce a condensed version of the appropriate length and to sign this hashed version. This has the advantage that the signing process is only performed once and that the message extension is restricted to one block length.

Clearly, for the signature to be effective, the hashed version must depend upon every bit of the message and must also depend upon the order in which they occur. The use of a bad hashing function may lead to many different meaningful messages having the same hashed version and, hence, to the possibility of removing a signature from the message for which it was intended and attaching it to another for which it is also valid. Thus great care is needed when selecting a hashing function. Finding suitable hashing functions is a difficult problem which is currently attracting the attention of a number of cryptographers.

8.5.3 Short messages

When the message is shorter than a single block then either a signed block can be appended to the message prior to transmission or the message may form an integral part of the signed block so that only the signed block needs to be transmitted. In the latter case it is likely to be easy to substitute fake messages unless some redundancy is introduced into the block to be signed. For these short messages the effectiveness of the signature scheme is likely to depend on the nature of this redundancy.

8.5.4 True signature schemes

In most signature schemes signed messages are sent directly by the signer to the receiver who verifies its validity. There is no need for the signature to be referred to a third party unless there is a dispute which, hopefully, is the exception rather than the rule. This type of scheme is called a true signature scheme. It requires the formulation of a disputes procedure and the appointment of accepted arbitrators, e.g. judges, but these arbitrators are not involved in the actual signing process. Since the arbitrator is not involved in the signing process that process needs careful selection. In particular it must be such that the arbitrator is able to come to a decision which the participants will accept as fair. (Note that this is not possible with the message authentication schemes based on conventional cryptography which were discussed in Section 2.) We will now look at two possibilities.

8.5.5 The use of public key cryptography

Digital signatures provide one of the most natural applications for public key systems, notably RSA and El Gamal.

In any public key system a user X has two keys : a public key p_X which determines an enciphering transformation and a private (secret) key s_X which determines a deciphering transformation. A message M may be sent to X in secret by enciphering it as the cryptogram $C = E_{p_x}(M)$. User X can decipher the cryptogram using his deciphering key D_{s_x} which must satisfy $D_{s_x}(E_{p_x}(M))$ $= M$ for all messages M. Both transformations E_{p_x} and D_{s_x} must be easy to perform and it must be computationally infeasible for anyone, from the knowledge of E_{p_x}. to derive D_{s_x}. Thus, with p_x made public, anyone can send to X a secret message which only X can decipher (using D_{s_x}).

If a public key system is such that the transformations E_{p_x} and D_{s_x} both act on the same set, then E_{p_x} and D_{s_x} are inverses of one another and $E_{p_x}(D_{s_x}(M)) = M$ for all messages M. When this is the case, user X may sign a message by forming the signature $S = D_{s_x}(M)$ and anyone can check the signature by computing $E_{p_x}(S)$ and comparing it with M. Note that since only X knows S_x this verification not only shows that the message M was unaltered but identifies X as the signer.

One obvious example of such a public key system is RSA. El Gamal, on the other hand, does not have this property, which means that the use of El Gamal for providing digital signatures is somewhat different to the decryption process.

8.5.6 Signatures by tamper-resistant modules

It is a fact that there is a (natural) separation between encryption and decryption in a public key cryptosystem which makes such systems candidates for digital signature schemes. Since each of the two functions has its own key, it is possible to be able to verify a signature (using 'encryption') without being able to generate a signature (which requires 'decryption'). For conventional systems there is not the same (natural) separation of keys. However if the encryption and decryption transformations were successfully separated then it would be possible to provide signatures using such a system. One way of achieving this separation is by physical means using tamper-resistant modules (TRMs).

Suppose we have a system where each user has a TRM which contains a key k_X for a conventional cryptosystem and that k_X determines an encryption transformation E_{k_x} and decryption transformation D_{k_x}. Suppose the key k_X could be communicated securely to all other TRMs and the modules were constructed so that while only X's TRM could perform E_{k_x} all other TRMs could only perform D_{k_x}. Then, provided that the tamper resistance of each module could be trusted, only X's TRM could generate a signature $S_X(M) = E_{k_x}(M)$ but any other TRM could verify a signature by computing $D_{k_x}(S)$ and checking whether or not $D_{k_x}(S) = M$.

It should be noted that, although this is the first example where it is explicitly stated that the security relies on tamper resistance, most digital signature schemes rely on some form of physical security. If, for example, we consider a scheme based on public key cryptography then the security relies on the sender X's ability to keep his secret key s_X secret. Great care is taken to ensure that s_X cannot be computed from knowledge of the algorithm and X's public key p_X. However this is not sufficient and X must also take steps to ensure that s_X is not exposed by physical means. Typical ways of achieving this are to use tamper resistant devices and/or to store all devices which hold s_X in physically secure locations.

8.5.7 Arbitrated signature schemes

There are many situations where it is not necessary for the receiver to check the signature on a received message. In fact it is frequently the case that signatures are only checked when a dispute arises.

An alternative to the use of true signature schemes is the arbitrated signature scheme in which signed messages can be sent only via a trusted third party called the arbitrator. The recipient is unable to verify the sender's signature directly, but is assured of its validity through the mediation of the arbitrator. The arbitrator must be trusted by both parties to play his role correctly and this gives the sender assurance that his signature will not be forged and the receiver assurance that the signatures he receives are valid. The arbitrator also plays the role of referee. He is trusted to resolve disputes (fairly) should they arise.

Arbitrated signature schemes are somewhat cumbersome and are often inconvenient to the users. However they do not need any complicated mathematical functions nor require significant processing overheads. As an example, we will illustrate a simple arbitrated signature scheme based on the use of DES. The fundamental assumption is that the arbitrator A is trusted by all participants. In this scheme each user X shares with A a secret key k_X which determines enciphering and deciphering transformations E_{k_x} and D_{k_x}.

One possible scheme involves user X sending messages to user Y via A. User X signs message M by encrypting it with key k_X and then sends M and $S = E_{k_x}(M)$ to A. The arbitrator A has key k_X and so can decrypt S to check that this gives M. A now sends $E_{k_y}(X,M,S)$ to user Y. User Y decrypts this to obtain X,M, and S. Provided the identity X and message M are acceptable to him, Y accepts S as the signature of M by X. In case of dispute, Y sends $E_{k_y}(X,M,S)$ to A who uses k_y to obtain X,M and S and then uses k_X to check that $E_{k_x}(M) = S$. Thus in this scheme Y cannot actually check X's signature directly. It is there solely to settle disputes. This arbitrated digital signature scheme relies heavily on the fact that both users X and Y must trust the arbitrator A. Signatures must be sent via A and only A

can verify signatures and resolve disputes. User X must trust A not to reveal key k_X and not to generate false signatures E_{k_x} (M). Similarly user Y must trust A to send E_{k_y} (X,M,S) only if E_{k_x} (M) = S. Furthermore both users must trust A to resolve disputes fairly. If the arbitrator acts as expected then X has an assurance that no-one can forge his signature and Y has an assurance that X cannot disavow his signature.

8.5.8 Standards?

ISO SC27 are currently discussing a number of proposals for a digital signature standard. These include:

- the use of RSA
- the NIST proposed DSS (using El Gamal)
- Schorr's scheme
- an adaptation of the Fiat–Shamir Identification Scheme
- ESIGN
- IS 9796 (Digital Signature scheme giving message recovery)

We will not include any technical details of any of these schemes. However we must point out that there are many considerations which might influence a user when deciding which scheme to use. One of them is, of course, the Standards, but others include the security level, implementation issues (both of which, hopefully, will influence the Standards Bodies!), licences/patents and public confidence. We also note that for a number of issues, such as security and implementation issues, it may not be necessary to have the 'best' scheme. Any scheme that is 'good enough' should be acceptable.

8.6 SOME APPLICATIONS

We conclude this paper by mentioning some of the more significant applications of digital signatures.

8.6.1 Key certification

One of the principal applications for digital signatures is in the provision of key 'certificates' for public key systems. This application is increasing in popularity because the current trend for key management of symmetric key systems is to use RSA for the distribution of top level keys, e.g. see CD 11166 Banking–Key management by means of asymmetric algorithms. If a public key system is to be used then it is absolutely crucial that everyone in the system should be confident that each user's public key is authentic. A common solution is for every user's public key to be signed by a Certification Authority; this signed key can then be stored in the public list of keys. Clearly this Certification Authority (CA) must be trusted to only sign valid keys, and everyone in the system must be able to verify the CA's signature. The key, together with the signature, is then usually referred to as a certificate for that user.

In practice it is necessary for the certificate to contain the name of the key owner as well as the public key itself. In addition the certificate may also contain extra information such as an expiry date. A typical certificate might then have the form

$$A, p_A, T, S_C (A, p_A, T)$$

where A is the name of the user, p_A is A's public key, T is the expiry date for p_A and S_C is the secret signature transformation of C_A.

Certification of public keys appears to be one of the most promising application areas for digital signatures. The 1988 version of the C.C.I.T.T. X.500 Directory Recommendations specifies how public key certificates may be stored in user directory entries; see in particular C.C.I.T.T. Recommendation X.509. The idea of digital signature based public key certificates has also been adopted to provide key management for Internet Electronic Mail security. Internet RFC 1114 specifies the use of an RSA signature for certifying RSA public keys.

C.C.I.T.T. Recommendation X.509 also makes provision for the case where more than one CA is used. This is done by allowing CAs to produce certificates for each other's public verification transformations. Sequences of such cross-certificates can be used to enable a user to obtain an authenticated copy of a CA's public verification transformation, and hence check a key certificate produced by that CA.

8.6.2 Authentication using digital signatures

In computer networks it is often necessary for communicating parties to verify one another's identity. Traditionally this is done by the use of passwords; however the security offered by passwords used in the standard way is very limited.

One alternative is the use of cryptographic authentication protocols, standards for which are now emerging. Some of the most important of these protocols are based on the use of digital signatures. C.C.I.T.T. Recommendation X.509 specifies three different protocols for authentication. These are all based on the use of digital signatures and the use of a cryptographic data structure called a token.

Like a certificate, a token is merely a series of data items with a signature appended. However, tokens are always specific to a single communication between two parties, i.e. when required a token is generated by an originator for transmission to a single recipient. The general form of the token specified in

X.509 for transmission from user A to user B is:

$$B, D, S_A(B, D)$$

where B is the name of the recipient, D is any data which is to be sent as part of the authentication protocol and S_A is A's secret signature transformation.

One of the protocols specified in X.509 (three-way authentication) has the following general form:

1 A sends to B: A, B, R_A, $S_A(B, R_A)$ where R_A is a random number.
2 B verifies the signature and checks that B's name is in the token.
3 B sends to A: A, B, R_A, R_B, $S_B(A, R_A, R_B)$ where R_B is another random number.
4 A verifies the signature, checks that A's name is in the token and checks for the presence of R_A (protecting against replays).
5 A sends to B: A, B, R_B, $S_A(B, R_B)$.
6 B verifies the signature, checks that B's name is in the token and checks for the presence of R_B (protecting against replays).

At the end of this process A and B are convinced of each other's identity.

There are many other applications for digital signatures (for instance Northern Telecom's secure telephone system for use with ISDN). Furthermore, methods not involving RSA are also being implemented.

9 Network Encryption Management

Vince Gallo
Airtech Computer Security

9.1 INTRODUCTION

Computers do not do very much 'computing'. Their main tasks tend to be translation and presentation of data and expansion of simple requests into compound commands. They act as an agent on behalf of a human who is incapable of expressing their wishes or accessing the data they require unaided. This use is maximised when the computer acts as an interface into the largest possible pool of resources and many companies have adopted this with enthusiasm. Large machines can be located wherever there is a suitable building, data can be located close to its source, and the users of the machines or data can do so from their normal place of work or when 'on the road'. A wide variety of machinery connected over wide areas will use few dedicated links, rather the need is for any site to be able to exchange data with any other site. Packet switching is therefore a popular method of connection.

The features of packet switching that makes it attractive for large and disparate networks include the ability to:

- establish any node to node connection;
- re-route of communications as required;
- use third party cables or networks over long distances;
- present data to a network to be sent wherever is required.

Unfortunately these are exactly the sort of details that can make the network insecure.

Any node to other node connection.

> You may often not wish EVERYBODY to be able to obtain connection to your nodes.

Simple re-routing of communications.

> Are you sure that you want your data re-routed? Where to? Across what links?

Use of third party cables or networks over long distances.

> As soon as third parties are used to convey data you are reliant on their procedures or the integrity of their employees.

Data presented to a network can be sent wherever it is required.

> The requirement is normally the legitimate destination, but switches are very good at replication data streams and very poor at deciding whose requirements they should meet.

Networks are useful, probably indispensable, to modern business users but they leave the information vulnerable to eavesdropping, corruption or alteration and masquerade. These attacks can lead to prosecution, blackmail or poor bargaining position. Competitors may benefit from product or research information. Decisions may be based on incorrect data.

9.2 CRYPTOGRAPHIC PROTECTION

Ideally one would like all the advantages a network to be utilised without the risk of security violations. It is tempting to suggest to the network provider that preventing theft or alteration of data is their responsibility. This is only practical where your data is of less importance than the average that they carry, for that is the level of protection that they will provide based on their own commercial judgement. Furthermore the legal arguments apportioning blame are of little use if you have already lost the market to your competitor, and the contractual limit of responsibility is likely to be quite low.

The correct view is that this is *your* data so *you* should look after it. This means that the protection should be external to the network connection removing reliance on any security, or lack of it, within the network.

There are several methods of doing this and arguably the best is to include cryptographic services within the applications. This is an example of the most difficult method to implement and is impossible to retro-fit.

In-line encryption has a number of advantages while also satisfying a number of the security requirements.

> In-line devices can encrypt data rendering it unintelligible. The decryption process is sensitive to altered or inserted traffic which will cause gross disruption to the output data stream.

> The ability to encrypt and decrypt is limited by access to the units and to keys. This provides effective closed-user groups that are under local control and not reliant on the network provider.

In-line devices can be added to conventional networks by providing a compatible, standard interface on both sides of the unit. This is necessary because security is often only considered after the rest of the system has been specified, supplied, or commissioned.

Separation of the functions allows communications devices to be selected on their own merits. This provides freedom of choice for initial installation or upgrade without any impact on, or by, security features.

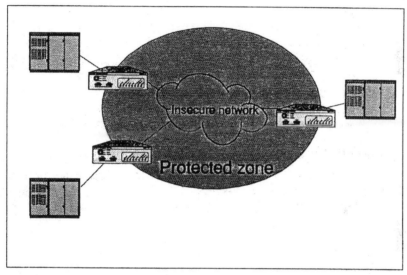

Figure 9.1 Encrypt the network from the outside

As with all cryptographic products the security is only effective if sound key distribution practices are followed. Failure to do so can leave weaknesses in a systems that are sometimeS more serious than no security at all, as the users are lulled into a false sense of security. Among the measures that should be adopted are :

• limitation of the devices that share keys (ideally this should be two);

• key life should be limited both in time and volume usage. In a packet switched system it is most appropriate if a new data key is used for each call placed over a SVC;

• keys should always either be encrypted or within a secure environment;

• humans should never have knowledge of key values.

9.3 KEY DISTRIBUTION

One of the most significant factors in a key management scheme is the method by which data keys are provided to each of the encryption devices. Several options exist that satisfy some or all of the criteria set out above. For each option the level of inconvenience can have a great effect on the cost and likelihood of adhering to, for example, key update frequency guidelines.

9.3.1 Manual token distribution for DEKs

A portable , secure, data storage device such as a smartcard can be loaded with a set of DEKs and taken to each device that requires a copy of them. After certain conditions, e.g. password verification, have been satisfied then the keys are surrendered by the token and accepted by the encryptor. Whenever new keys are required new tokens must be created and transported to all encryptors. Routine updates can be planned but remain expensive in time and travel costs. More problematic are any emergency updates that may be required following a suspected compromise of key material.

Current practice of running 'dark sites' make it almost impossible in some cases to visit equipment on a routine basis. Encryptors that need direct access must therefore either cause gross disruption to normal routine or, more likely, be located elsewhere and thus extend the unsecured section of the communications link.

9.3.2 Manual token distribution for KEKs

The scheme outlined above becomes more attractive if the frequency with which the manual distribution was required is reduced. This can be done by using the token content as keys as Key Encrypting Keys (KEKs) so that once they are in place DEKs, encrypted under a KEK, may be sent to the encryptors over the network. The bulk of the distribution is thus mechanised with less frequent KEK updates remaining a necessity. Unfortunately the times that such keys need to be moved are when a new node is introduced to the network, when an existing unit fails and needs to be replaced, or when some emergency key update is required. These are all times of greatest urgency or inconvenience and it is thus undesirable for there to be a need to send people around.

9.3.3 PKC distribution of KEKs

Once it has been accepted that DEKs may be transmitted over the network there should be no difficulty with doing the same for KEKs provided that suitable cryptographic precautions are taken. Public Key Cryptography, in particular RSA, provides a suitable algorithm. Two units can exchange public keys and the KEK may be then be encrypted and signed providing both secrecy and authenticity. The acceptability of unit public keys is controlled by a certification agency that is responsible for preparation of public key certificates so that units may trust each other without any prior exchange of data.

The hierarchy of certification agency, unit RSA keys, symmetric KEKs and finally DEKs allows frequent key updates to be performed without any need for human operators to be involved or for the transfer of physical tokens. The net result is that all of the key distribution criteria can be satisfied without incurring large operational costs.

9.3.4 Key management complexity

The attraction of a key hierarchy suitable for full electronic distribution is reduced somewhat if the full population of keys are considered. The quantity of keys involved for a small number of units ($N < 10$ say) is acceptable for humans as N^2 is still small. When the total number of units becomes large (thousands of units are commonly discussed) then the number of keys in existence can be very large. Certainly when frequent key updates are contemplated on this scale the task becomes too large to be managed directly by humans and probably by any single piece of hardware.

There is in place a large array of distributed intelligence, i.e. the encryptors themselves, and the task for each is reduced to the order of N rather than N^2. An additional benefit of using the units themselves is that the human operators are not involved with each key update so there is no natural limitation on the frequency of key changes.

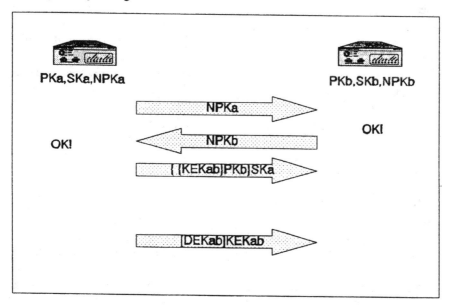

Figure 9.2 Key hierarchy

What has evolved from these considerations is a system that comprises N encryptors, each of which is an autonomous key distribution centre. This ensures that there is enough capacity and resilience in the system.

9.4 OPERATIONAL DIFFICULTIES

The ease of interfacing is a significant factor in the justification of in-line type devices as existing communications links can be broken at a suitable standard protocol interface and the units inserted. Neither the host (DTE) or the network need to know of, nor should they notice, any change.

Provided everything works as it was designed to then there will be no problems, but as every network operator is aware this is not a permanent situation. The simple fact that additional equipment exists will increase the chances of something failing. The fact that the encryptors are in-line means that the result of a failure is likely to be a severe disruption to communications.

Very few technical features are created without some initial need that must be satisfied, or some benefit accruing. Recently all major suppliers of communications equipment have been adding network management facilities to their devices. Why has so much money been spent on additional software and increased processor capability where neither results in any improved baseline functionality? The answer is that large communications networks are 'impossible' to control without central management facilities.

The requirements are for initialisation, re-configuring, diagnostics, audit or traffic flow analysis and fault reporting. Mostly a central management station will send commands, information or requests to a remote device but remote units can also send un-prompted status reports if a situation arises that requires intervention.

When encryptors are considered as 'just another piece of communications equipment' then it becomes obvious that they cause the same difficulties and therefore require similar management facilities. It has taken us suppliers a while to come to this conclusion but we have got there eventually.

9.5 CRYPTO DEVICE MANAGEMENT

All of the rationale that justifies central management of communications equipment is applicable to encryption devices, and in some cases more so. The largest logistical problem of network management is that most expertise is concentrated on a few sites and most of those at the periphery are users with little understanding of details. Awareness of cryptographic products is at present less common than that of communications, reducing the chances to almost zero that anyone other than a central corps of experts will be able to manipulate the devices. Without remote management capability the members of this central group could need to travel to the devices which would be far too slow and expensive.

It is worth considering what aspects of security devices need manipulation and whether these are suitable for centralised control.

9.5.1 Control of key update strategy

The key hierarchy discussed above provides a workable mechanism for electronic distribution, and using each unit to take care of its own needs allows this to be automated. Implementing such an automated scheme requires that each device be given an update strategy which it should follow. While there is no human involvement in the pursuit of such a strategy, there is a requirement to inform the unit in the first place, and occasionally there may be a need to alter the key update pattern. This is particularly true if a compromise is suspected where the units involved would be instructed to execute an immediate key update and then proceed as normal.

9.5.2 Communications configuration

Initial device configuration will always be required where the protocol is other than trivial. A standard set-up, derived during the initial device trials, will be adequate for most units on a single network. Alterations will be required if switches from a number of manufacturers are used, or if higher speed lines are installed. Changes may also be considered in order to 'tune' the network for increased throughput or reduced delays.

9.5.3 New nodes

Few networks are static and new nodes may be added, while others may be removed. Nodes that have some security requirement will need to have a new encryptor added which will need to be set up. Initially the node should be commissioned without the encryptor, then with the device in-line but operating in plain text only mode. Once the equipment is operating satisfactorily then particular links from the new node to others on the network may be switched to enciphered mode by informing each encryptor about its peer. This process involves updating information, setting the encrypt mode flag for the peer NUA configuration in the units at both ends of a virtual circuit.

Other node specific details that may need updating concern the way that units should handle calls to and from particular, or unknown, addresses. The options may be to block incoming or outgoing calls, or there may be time-of-day restrictions placed on these events. All of these details may need to be reconfigured at some stage.

9.5.4 Audit trail access

The benefit of multiple autonomous devices is that there is a high degree of resilience and each processor has a reasonable degree of complexity. One certain disadvantage is that there will be an activity log, or audit trail, in each device. These will need to be inspected to ensure that key change strategies are being executed as requested. Other details that may prove useful are logs of calls detailing address, time and duration as well as particular interest in calls to or from unknown addresses. Data contained in such logs can provide indications of attempted or actual breaches of security, usually by internal staff.

It is necessary to be able to upload the log details to a single central database so that they may all be examined, in particular in relation to each other, to help identify patterns of attack on the network as a whole.

9.5.5 Fault finding

Without doubt the most important aspect of centralised management is the ability to keep the network running when some devices have failed. Communication switches need to be programmed to re-route data around faulty units, perhaps making use of stand-by circuits. Even if there is no way to jury-rig the network, it is essential that the scope of any failure be assessed so that an appropriate repair team can be dispatched. In the event that users, or devices, are reporting an inability to connect to a particular address then it is important that the culprit be identified. There could be a fault on the switch, the encryptor could have failed or the host DTE may be down. The ability to place a distinct call to the encryptor itself, even if the host is not working, will help analyse which unit has failed.

Cryptographic devices are responsible for secure storage of secret key material and therefore often include electronics for tamper detection. The result of an attack on the unit will be for it to destroy all internal key values and to raise an alarm. This is directly equivalent to equipment that self-diagnose some hardware failure and it is therefore beneficial if the unit is able to contact the management centre to report the alarm. If the encryptor has failed, perhaps the keys were erased because the unit was shaken or disconnected, then it would be useful if it could be re-commissioned without the need for a site visit.

9.5.6 Dark sites

A practical justification for remote management is that a la rge number of computer and communication establishments are now run as 'dark sites'. This removes the cost of human oriented facilities as well as increasing the inherent security of such sites. Unfortunately there cannot be any equipment in such locations that requires local control. It must be remotely managed.

This list of controls required over encryption equipment shows clearly the need for some form of remote management. In almost all cases there would be cost savings, but sometimes it is simply impossible, without such features, to add encryption to a particular network layout. Many of these features would be applicable to line encryptors but network level devices such as X.25 encryptors have an increased need to be remotely manageable as well as a suitable channel for such control. X.25 is designed to allow multiple virtual circuits to co-exist on a single physical link, and so there is no fundamental problem of management control over a SVC in addition to the host to network virtual circuits being encrypted.

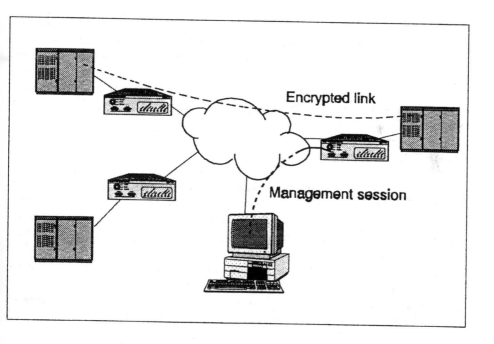

Figure 9.3 Remote management

9.6 NETWORK MANAGEMENT STANDARDS

A number of proprietary management protocols have been designed and implemented leading to incompatibility between equipment from different suppliers. The role of standards bodies is to set a common mechanism whereby mixed vendor networks can be managed from a single centre. The main drive behind the emerging standards has been to maximise the chances of controlling any particular device in the shortest time scale. To this end a number of 'difficult' problems were recognised and consciously shelved for subsequent revisions.

While accepting that the purpose of central management is to enable remote control of a device it must be recognised that encryptors are security enforcing devices. Free control over such devices must therefore not be possible. Far from the standards bodies' aim to ease the management of all devices, the encryptors must place very strict controls on who is allowed to manage them. The only effective way of doing this is to introduce cryptographic protection on the management protocol, and this is exactly the sort of 'difficulty' that has been delayed from the standards discussions. Suppliers of this type of equipment cannot afford to wait. Control over the configuration of an encryption device would include the ability to redefine particular addresses as plain text routes and clearly there needs to be a restriction on who may wield this power. The subject device is only aware of a command, and without strong cryptographic checks it has no way of confirming the validity of either the origin of a message or its contents.

Special needs governing the control of security equipment go some way towards justifying a proprietary management system but do not justify complete isolation. The need of a large communication system manager is for centralised control. Just positioning all management consols in one building, or one room, is not enough; the information and control needs to be integrated into a single workstation. It is possible to achieve this, but only if the suppliers of the security equipment make the commitment to support standard interfaces. The arguments about secure control apply to the encryptors but not to the management centre itself, so a feasible topology would be for the central management centre to interrogate or instruct the encryptor management centre which would then manipulate the encryption devices.

The security implications of this should be considered carefully. The trust by the encryptors of their management centre is based on cryptography while the management centre only trusts the user by following a logon or similar authentication process. How should this trust be extended to a second management computer and so to its operator? This is the point at which pragmatism must take over from dogma. Both management processors are likely to be located in close proximity, probably in a secure room with entry control. There is a high degree of responsibility placed on the communications network managers and they already have total control over the network configuration. Providing them with the means to control encryption units as well is likely to be acceptable.

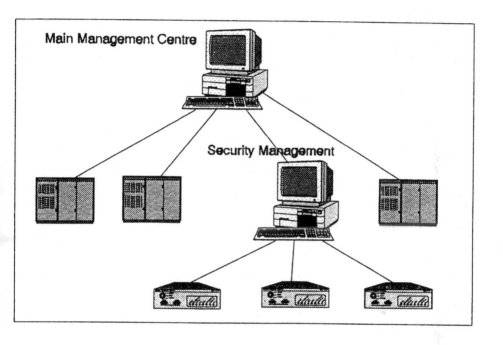

Figure 9.4 Total management

9.7 CONCLUSION

Networks are a vital part of modern computer systems and one on which most institutions are dependent. Data transferred by many networks is vulnerable to a number of attacks, the effects of which can be serious. Encryption offers reasonable protection at low cost of ownership provided appropriate key distribution schemes are implemented and that the resulting management issues are addressed. Given the presence of adequate computing power in the encryption devices to support management protocols, centralised control of all forms of communication equipment should now include the security equipment as well as the data transmission devices. Users are best placed to express their needs as they understand best the business requirements and their own environment. It is the responsibility of security equipment suppliers to justify peculiar restrictions, but sooner rather than later encryption equipment must be built to fit in with the rest of an interoperative world.

10 Computer Crime: Law and Regulation – Protection and Prosecution

Wendy R London
Cameron Markby Hewitt

10.1 INTRODUCTION

The introduction of anything new into today's world often seems to be accompanied by new ways of 'beating the system'. This is especially true, as we well know, in the computer/high tech area. Computers, when in the wrong hands, provide a low-cost and often easy route to committing crimes, either within the target computer system itself or through use of the computer to commit other crimes. In this paper, we will be looking at some of these crimes and what legislatures have done to punish them. We will also look at what companies can and should do to protect themselves and communicate to their staffs their obligations and responsibilities in this area, and at the effect of undesirable high tech behaviour on the development of new technologies. First, let's turn to adopting a working definition of 'computer crime'.

10.2 COMPUTER CRIME: DEFINITION AND SCOPE

The OECD offers us the following definition of 'computer crime':

> Any illegal, unethical, or unauthorised behaviour involving automatic processing and/or transmission of data.

It is a definition which incorporates crimes involving the computer itself as well as the use of a computer as an instrument to commit a crime not specifically relating to computing. The following criminal activities fall within this definition:

- unauthorised computer manipulation; fraud;
- computer theft;
- theft of data, software and semi-conductor chips;
- computer sabotage;

- theft of services;
- unauthorised access to DP systems;
- traditional offences assisted by DP (see our hospital example, below);
- computer-related infringements of privacy.

For an example of the use of a computer as an instrument to commit a further crime, we can turn to the misguided person who turns off or interferes with a computerised hospital supervision system with the result that the patient dies, an act of murder. Thus, the crime need not be perpetrated on the computer itself, but can be designated a 'computer crime' where a computer is only 'merely involved'. This leads to some extremely frightening possibilities as soon as we start thinking the ways in which we use computers today, including:

- to store, manipulate and process information;

- to effect various operations such as
  - transferring funds
  - running air traffic control
  - measuring dosages in hospitals
  - operating robots on a production line;

- to carry out various commercial activities including
  - performing stock control, automatic re-ordering, etc.
  - transacting business on the Stock Exchange
  - booking reservations on airplanes and in hotels.

Just think for a brief moment about disaffected employees in this country alone who have:

- re-programmed a robot so as to cause a shop floor worker to suffer serious injuries;
- accessed a tour operator's network so as to swamp it with false orders;
- caused mail shots to be sent automatically to thousands of non-customers;

or about the hacker who deleted an architect's design files and the other one who deleted a year's worth of research at a university.

Linkages with organised crime also have been uncovered, often in the areas of money laundering and the management and transfer of illegally acquired assets. In addition, computers have been the target of, or used for, unauthorised surveillance. Computer crime is a serious threat to every organisation which uses automated systems. It is a threat which will grow with time, and which will be accompanied by an ever-increasing potential for damage and loss. The growth of potential danger is a function of:

- the increasing use of, and dependency on, computer technology in all facets of society; a growth which in some quarters has significantly outpaced the development of the underlying social, legal and political infrastructure;
- the increasing interdependence of computer systems ;
- the growth in the number of users, in large part due to erosion of the mystique associated with computers and the lower cost of computing;
- the increasing ease with which people can gain access to computer systems.

Developing countries are particularly vulnerable to computer threats and dangers because of their reliance on high technology to kick start their economies. In addition, they run an especially high risk in terms of physical, economic and social costs should their systems be attacked.

We unfortunately have no accurate measure of the extent of the damage which can be attributed to computer crime because of the reluctance of victims to report their experiences, a reluctance which is characterised by (a) an unwillingness to disclose their vulnerability, (b) a fear of the effect on customers and clients (especially banks and other financial institutions), (c) a general feeling that the authorities would be unable to assist in any event (both in terms of the problems related to tracing the offender and the lack of expertise which the authorities can offer), and (d) recognition that recovery of losses is unlikely, either directly or through insurance cover.

It is interesting to note, though, that there appears to be a growing confidence that the authorities *will* prosecute offenders who are reported, at least in the UK.

Reporting also may be a second choice for companies who prefer to rely on their own internal procedures. This may be due to the probable high cost of bringing a court action and the problems which an investigation carries with it, i.e. immobilising or removing systems, staff unrest, damage to software, etc.

The *cost* of computer crime is also difficult to assess. Losses relating to computer-initiated fraud are perhaps the simplest to quantify because, generally, there is direct financial damage. In cases of hacking, however, there may be no financial damage caused. Software piracy is another difficult aspect of computer crime to calculate since no one really knows for sure just how many copies of **Kings Quest** really have been made.

Guesstimates of damage can be made based on the nature of the organisation, at least in relative terms. For example, a firm with desks full of unprotected PCs on a network is probably more vulnerable to computer viruses than is a firm reliant on its protected mainframe. Similarly, a financial services house is more likely to be targeted than is a company manufacturing widgets.

It is up to governments to legislate in the field of computer crime.

10.3 LEGISLATION AND REGULATION: THE UNITED KINGDOM

Reinterpreting 'old law' to suit computer and computer-related crimes has proven to be an exercise as fruitful as pushing a square peg into a round hole in many jurisdictions. For example, theft of information has proven to be a totally different concept from theft of a car or a sterling silver toothpick because information is *intangible*; it is not property in the classical criminal law sense where someone (the perpetrator) can physically pick it up and permanently deprive the victim of its use.[1]

Furthermore, the traditional definition of 'property' imputes a notion of *exclusivity*, i.e. the property belongs to one person, and one person only. Information, on the other hand, is by its very nature generally shared.

One need only look at the treatment of intellectual *property* rights to get a sense of this: even IPRs award the creator rights only within certain time and geographic boundaries.[2]

Prior to enactment of the Computer Misuse Act 1990, cases of hacking and misuse were for the most part brought under the Theft Act 1968. However, charges brought under the Act were not very successful where computers were used as the instruments of fraud or theft. Fraud didn't work because there was no deception of a human being (under section 15), and theft often didn't work because no 'property' was stolen (under section 1). Where possible, cases were brought under section 17, false accounting, or under conspiracy to defraud where two or more people were involved.

In addition, the Law Commission saw that hacking would have a deleterious effect on the growth, development and use of computer systems if users and potential users could not be assured that the law would serve to protect such systems. Similarly, the Law Commission rejected all suggestions that hackers were doing users a favour by testing systems by hacking into them.

Thus it was felt that there was indeed justification for enacting legislation covering the misuse of computers.

As in many jurisdictions, the UK legislators quite properly – in my view – concluded that a number of new criminal offences would have to be created in respect of computer and computer-related crime rather than trying to force the

---

[1] Note, however, jurisdictions such as the many American states which have brought computer data within the ambit of traditional definitions of property by defining data and trade secrets as 'things of value' so as to retrofit computer crime into the traditional crime of larceny.

[2] As such, most continental countries treat misappropriation of someone else's data or the illegal abstraction of secret information under special provisions dealing with the betrayal or misappropriation of trade secrets. This approach comports with the information theory which rejects the *static* property theory and instead relies on the *relationship* and *entitlement* theories.

Unfortunately, the Law Commission in considering the need for legislation dealing with computer misuse stopped short at criminalising the initial unauthorised access and left open the troublesome issue of *property rights in information*. Critics have raised the questions as to whether confidential information stored in computers should be brought within the definition of 'property' as found in the Theft Acts and whether our criminal law should be extended to punish the unauthorised removal of trade secrets.

interpretation of, or extending, old offences, some dating back to the beginning of the realm.

An example of the problems encountered in applying old law can be found in *Cox v. Riley*[3] where it was held that the (then) existing criminal law was sufficiently comprehensive to deal with damage to data where the medium holding the data has been damaged (e.g. by physical destruction or by the introduction of viruses or worms), but that criminal or unauthorised modification to the data itself was not covered by that law. In other words, the Criminal Damage Act 1971, by virtue of section 1, could be applied where *tangible property* such as disks, tapes or hard disks were destroyed or damaged, but that the Act could not be applied where there was alteration or erasure of data, even though such acts can cause substantial loss and physical danger (e.g. haywire robots and sending two planes to the same place at the same time).

Let us now turn to our own main legislative provision in the area of computer crime, the Computer Misuse Act 1990.

10.4 THE COMPUTER MISUSE ACT 1990

The three offences, which were recommended by the Law Commission in its October 1989 report and which form the three main offences of the CMA as enacted are:

- the basic hacking offence;
- the ulterior intent offence (hacking plus something else); and
- unauthorised modification of computer material.

10.4.1 The basic hacking offence

In its 1989 report,[4] the Law Commission concluded that deterrents to the invasion of computer systems is a proper public goal and recommended that hacking be criminalised. The rationale cited by it included the following factors:

- the actual losses and costs incurred by computer owners whose systems are breached;
- the fact that unauthorised entry may be preliminary to the commission of general criminal offences; and
- that computer owners and users may feel insecure without protection from the law.

---

[3] *Cox v Riley* turned on tangible damage to the medium on which the data was stored under the Criminal Damage Act 1971. In this case, data was stored on a plastic circuit card.

[4] The Law Commission, **Criminal Law: Computer Misuse** (Law Comm. no. 186) (London: HMSO Cm 819, 1989).

Messrs Gold and Schifreen highlighted the need to enact legislation which would make hacking punishable. They were prosecuted under the Forgery and Counterfeiting Act 1981 for alleged computer hacking, but were acquitted on the basis that, as required by the Act, no *person* was induced to respond to the input of the Personal Identification Number since it was the *computer* which responded. In other words, Gold and Schifreen had not created a 'false instrument' as required by the Act by using a Personal Identification Number.

Thus hacking *per se* was criminalised by section 1 of the CMA. Under this offence, a person is guilty if, under section 1(1):

(a) he causes a computer to perform any function with intent to secure access to any program or data held in any computer;
(b) the access he intends to secure is unauthorised; and
(c) he knows at the time when he causes the computer to perform the function that this is the case.

Section 1(2) goes on to say that:

(2) the intent a person has to have to commit an offence under this section need not be directed at
(a) any particular program or data;
(b) a program or data of any particular kind; or
(c) a program or data held in any particular computer.

In a rather creative stab at drafting, the language used in the Act, 'causes a computer to perform any function', very neatly gets around the problem of having to define 'access', a stumbling block which has caused problems in the United States. In other words, hacking is an actionable offence whether the hacker gains access or not. However, merely looking at a screen is not actionable; the hacker must cause some function to be performed by the computer. This phrase effectively covers all degrees of hacking, i.e. everything from complete access, where the hacker roams around the system, to where he reaches only the menu.

A different approach has been taken in France and in several American states to the problem of using a computer but committing no further crime: the crime of 'computer trespass' covers serious as well as nursery hacking.

It is also interesting to note that the UK did not adopt the approach found in many continental systems which require victims to prove that they were not contributorily negligent, i.e. that they had a security system in place. In the UK it was felt that hacking itself needed to be criminalised, that this particular law did not need to protect any given information (which is, in part at least, covered by the Data Protection Act 1984).

As with every crime, the perpetrator's state of mind is at issue. State of mind may apply to the seriousness of the crime (e.g. the difference between murder and manslaughter) or whether there is a crime at all (e.g. the difference between borrowing and theft).

Under the hacking offence of the CMA, the prosecution must prove that the alleged hacker:

- knew that he was not authorised to access the computer system; and
- intended to secure access or obtain information about a program or data.

Recklessness, carelessness and inattentiveness are not enough. However, as we saw above, an offence will be deemed to be committed if, after having gained access, the hacker realises what's 'on offer' and goes and takes a look.

In order to prove that unauthorised access has taken place, it is strongly recommended that an access control system with a secure log be implemented so that all significant events can be recorded. The ability to prove that access was attempted or successfully made from a particular workstation at a given time may be crucial in proving that an offence has taken place.

Hacking carries a fine of up to £2,000 and/or not more than six months in jail. As a summary offence, it is triable only in the Magistrates Courts.

What is gapingly absent from the Act is a definition of 'computer'.

10.4.2 The ulterior intent offence

The ulterior intent offence (section 2) constitutes an aggravated form of the basic hacking offence. In other words, section 2 applies when there is an intent to commit a further crime arising out of hacking into a computer system. Section 2(4) does not require that the perpetrator actually carry out the further offence or indeed that the further offence is possible; he only need envisage it. Also, where the further offence is to be carried out, it does not need to be carried out at the same time as the hacking offence, but can be carried out at any time in the future (section 2(3)). For example, information found out during the hacking offence might be used for insider dealing six months down the line when the 'event' occurs.

Therefore, the hacker can be convicted on an *attempted* section 2 offence as well as on actually having completed it. (Having said that, it may prove to be difficult to get a section 2 conviction if the information hasn't as yet been used.)

Proof is more difficult in the ulterior intent offence than in the hacking offence. Best proof will lie in further action having been taken – for example, the creation of a bank account or the consummation of trading in given shares.

The ulterior intent offence is triable on summary conviction, in which case the punishment is not more than six months in prison and/or a fine, or in Crown Court upon indictment, in which case the punishment is not more than five years in prison and/or a fine. The choice of 'five years' was not accidental: it means that the police can rely on their coercive powers of searching the alleged perpetrator's premises and seizing suspect goods during the process.

10.4.3 Unauthorised modification of computer material

The modification offence under section 3 covers a wide variety of activities:

- erasure of data;
- modification of data;
- putting worms, logic bombs and viruses into circulation;
- preventing an authorised user from gaining access to his own system (note the Florida statute which even goes so far as to punish behaviour which prevents a programmer from reaching work (Fla. Stat. Ann. section 815.06)).

The offence itself requires that modification was or would have been caused (had the suspect succeeded), that the modification was unauthorised, that the person knew that the modification was unauthorised, and that the suspect intended to impair the operation of the computer in some way through the modification (section 3(1)). In this offence, the prosecution need prove only that the *intent* to impair was present (section 3(2)); the prosecution need not prove that the activities were directed at any particular computer, program or data, or at any particular modification or modification of any kind (section 3(3)).

The prosecution must prove, with respect to *intent*, that the suspect knew that the modification he intended to cause was unauthorised (section 3(4)).

10.5 PROCEDURAL ISSUES

10.5.1 Prosecution

Prosecution continues to be an extremely difficult problem in the area of computer crime. One of the biggest problems is proof. There are several aspects of this problem which are particularly thorny.

One aspect involves the sheer size and complexity of the systems which constitute the focus of the investigation. These factors alone can make it difficult to prove precisely what damage has been done by the offender. A fairly high level of expertise is required for the investigating authorities to understand enough about what computers and networks do so as to be able to identify and describe the problems which are the subject of the complaint. These actions need to be taken quickly so that data is not erased or altered in any way. In addition, investigators should have sufficient expertise to be able to get into systems without the assistance of others, and to find and save the data in a manner in which it can be used in evidence in court.

A second problem revolves around the expertise of the hacker himself. The hacker is usually sufficiently 'talented' so that he will conceal his actions, e.g. through the erasure of data or the introduction of logic bombs.

Another problem that is likely to arise is the likelihood that defence counsel will insist on proof that the computer was working properly.[5] This ploy, as we can easily foresee, will prove to be extremely time consuming and may in fact lead to the failure of an otherwise successful prosecution.

Unless done by an insider, unauthorised access is most likely to be made over the public telephone networks. This causes two problems. The first lies in the difficulty in establishing a relationship between the offence and a suspect, a fairly technical issue. The second involves an issue which undoubtedly will be tested in the courts, and that is whether evidence obtained through traces on the telecommunications networks is admissible in court – or even whether tracing is legal at all.[6]

Problems in prosecution also may arise because of the very laws which the authorities are charged with upholding. Data protection laws, as we know, are designed to protect individuals from unauthorised access to their personal data. Thus, is it permissible to give the police and other authorities the power to access data stored in computer systems without the consent of the person to whom the data belongs, even for the purpose of solving a crime and/or prosecuting an offender?

Fortunately, procedural criminal law provides the way forward for doing so by introducing safeguards for exercising this power, just as is done in the realm of non-computer crime. Search and seizure of computer systems are allowable as long as the tests of reasonableness and proportionality are applied at each step and as long as the appropriate limitations for searches are respected.

10.5.2 Investigation and evidence

A special unit – the Computer Crime Unit (CCU) – was established by New Scotland Yard in 1985 to investigate cases of computer crime, including the coordination of all cases involving computer viruses. The unit is composed of detectives experienced in investigating frauds and the use of computers in investigative work. However, fraud, forgery and other classical crimes do not fall within the mandate of this unit, therefore most of its work is concerned with crimes where the computer itself is the target. Experts, both from within the Metropolitan Police Force and from outside, may be called upon by the CCU to assist in investigations. The CCU liaises with the telephone carriers (e.g. BT and Mercury).

---

[5] *See* section 69(1)(b) of the Police and Criminal Evidence Act 1984 which states that
  at all material times the computer was operating properly, or if not, that any respect in which it was not operating properly or was out of operation was not such as to affect the production of the document or the accuracy of its contents.
The same provision is found in the Civil Evidence Act 1968, section 5(2)(c). In both cases, if the computer is found to be infected with a computer virus, any documentary evidence taken from that computer might be ruled admissible.

[6] *See* Interception of Communications Act 1985.

The CCU has jurisdiction in London; victims outside London should contact their local police force who may then contact the CCU for assistance.

Investigation into computer crimes usually must be done by experts, and in all cases should follow a procedure designed to preserve, protect and identify what is likely to become significant evidence. The first step is to isolate and render inoperable the computer that has been used as an instrument in the crime or is itself the target of the crime. At the same time, the computer should be described in terms of its make, model, configuration, and operating system. Investigating police may require that the files also be isolated and protected from further modification and/or destruction, and that drives, disks, tapes etc. be removed for forensic examination. Particular problems may be encountered if there is a need to seize and transport a mainframe: the police generally will copy the relevant files to disk and rely on an expert to help in their interpretation.

In the UK, the Police and Criminal Evidence Act 1984 (PACE) says that a policeman has an explicit power to investigate a computer which is present on the premises.[7] Furthermore, section 14(1) of the CMA empowers a judge to issue search warrants for offences believed to have been committed under section 1 of the Act: these warrants empower the police to 'enter and search the premises, using such reasonable force as is necessary'. Materials which are privileged and excluded under section 9(2) of the Act are excluded from these search warrants. 'Premises' is defined as including land, buildings, movable structures, vehicles, vessels, aircraft and hovercraft under section 14(5).

10.5.3 Courts and juries

Computers and the things people do with them are complex and not part of the everyday experience of most people (in the way driving a car or operating a microwave oven are). Computers are particularly complex and overwhelming objects for most judges and counsel; danger lies in the judge or lawyer whose attempts to construe the law end in an unexpected result or at very least, a misinterpretation of the law as happened in *Cropp*.[8]

Accordingly, much more investment needs to be made in order to educate judges and the authorities so that they can carry out their responsibilities as expected.

---

[7] Police and Criminal Evidence Act (1984), sections 19(4) and (20).

[8] We are probably all familiar with the case of Sean Cropp by now. Sean Cropp was an ex-employee who returned to the company as a customer and when the back of the sales assistant was turned, allegedly entered a discount on the sale of the goods he was purchasing by inserting an erroneous number on the computer. He was acquitted by the Snaresbrook Crown Court on the basis that no offence was committed under section 1(1) (the offence under which he was charged) because *a second computer terminal was not used in the commission of the offence.* The Judge held that if the allegations against Cropp were in fact true, they *were* chargeable under section 3 (modification), an offence which was not pleaded in court but which had been included in the original indictment. In June 1992, the Court of Appeals overturned this judgement, finding fault with the Judge's interpretation of the Computer Misuse Act. *See also* note 14, *infra.*

10.5.4 International implications

Computer crime is not an activity that is limited to a particular road or village or county or even country. Computer crime is mobile crime and is a relatively low cost way of effecting crime from thousands of miles away. Computer crime does not respect national boundaries, or even time zones or vast bodies of water. It is completely oblivious to all barriers and boundaries.

Under section 4 of the CMA, a suspect can be prosecuted not only if the victim or the suspect is in the United Kingdom (and note that the CMA applies to the whole of the UK) but also if there is a significant link with the UK. Section 15 allows for the extradition of a suspect (a) where an ulterior intent or modification offence has been committed, (b) where there is a conspiracy to commit any such offence, and (c) where there is an *attempt* to commit an offence under section 3.

On a broader scale, it is important that countries agree on their approach to and cooperation in the definition, reporting, investigation and prosecution of computer crime. Specifically, the Eighth UN Congress on the Prevention of Crime and the Treatment of Offenders: Computer-Related Crimes[9] has called for a concerted international strategy which involves:

- modernisation of national criminal laws including
  - harmonisation of substantive law
  - harmonisation of procedural law (including proof, jurisdiction to prosecute, etc.)
  - the implementation of adequate investigative powers
  - the application of adequate admissibility of evidence rules
  - laws requiring the forfeiture of illegally acquired assets
  - harmonisation;
- improvement of computer security and prevention measures (with the caveat that personal privacy, human rights and fundamental freedoms are protected);
- development of measures to sensitise the public, the judiciary and law enforcement agencies to the problems which exist and the ways of preventing them;
- provision of adequate training for judges, officials and agencies responsible for the prevention, investigation, prosecution and adjudication of economic and computer-related crimes;
- elaboration, in collaboration with interested organisations, of the rules of ethics in the use of computers and the teaching of these rules as part of training in informatics;

---

[9] As reported in Bawden, *International Symposium on the Prevention and Prosecution of Computer Crime*, [1990 - 91] 7 CLSR 7.

- adoption of policies for the victims of computer-related crimes, including
  - restitution of illegally obtained assets; and
  - measures to encourage victims to report.

In addition, the UN Congress called for mutual assistance on criminal matters and an investment in research and analysis to find new ways to deal with computer crime.

The economic stakes are large. If mutual understanding and harmonisation are not achieved, data havens will result and barriers will be erected which will thwart the free flow of information. Barriers could result in companies being unable to export their goods and services to countries which have lower degrees of legal protection for computers than their own (a threat which is perceived as extremely serious by the EC in its quest to establish the Single Market) and in governments restricting data flow between their country and others which have less-developed laws, especially in the area of Data Protection.

10.6 OTHER ISSUES NOT DIRECTLY OR OBVIOUSLY ADDRESSED BY THE COMPUTER MISUSE ACT

10.6.1 Interaction with the Data Protection Act 1984

The words 'unauthorised' and 'access' found in section 1(b) of the CMA also can be found in Schedule 1 of the Data Protection Act 1984 which urges data holders to take 'appropriate security measures...against unauthorised access to, or alteration, disclosure or destruction of, personal data'.

10.6.2 Bulletin boards

The use of bulletin boards as a means of dealing in passwords and giving advice on how to hack into any given system constitutes an offence under the Computer Misuse Act.

10.6.3 Misuse of computer time and services

Since it is not a criminal offence to use your firm's electric typewriter for personal business (although I am sure many office managers would like to make it one!), why should the use of the firm's computers for the same purpose be made into an offence? Hence, the absence of such an offence from the UK statute. However, it is not inconceivable that some activities would fall under the CMA, e.g. accessing the firm's copy of WordPerfect without authorisation (hacking) or using up a substantial amount of processing power and thereby causing corruption to stored data (unauthorised modification to data).

10.6.4 Fraud

Fraud has proven to be a difficult issue for legislators in all jurisdictions. Under most definitions, fraud turns on the deceit of the human mind. Since it is not (yet) possible to deceive a machine, fraud in itself is not an actionable offence under computer crime statutes. However, there is clearly a recognition of the link between unauthorised access and fraud, a link which the Law Commission addressed.

The Law Commission stated in its Working Paper on Computer Misuse that the general criminal law should be adequate to cover fraud with one exception, and that is computer fraud.[10] It saw the most common variety of 'computer fraud' as input fraud, i.e. a fraud committed by insiders (authorised users) who seek to create false accounts, etc. One year later in its report,[11] the Law Commission recommended that changes – which it characterised as minor – be made to the law to cover computer fraud. By doing so, the Law Commission expressed concern over the growth of international computer fraud, due in large part to the ease with which modern technology facilitates the international movement of money and obligations.[12] For example, it is very easy to plan a fraud in one country to be carried out by the use of a remote computer in another.

Even apart from the arguments of whether it is legally possible to label an offence as 'computer fraud', there are two situations where a crime does arise. The first involves the inchoate crime of conspiracy: although a charge of fraud may not be supported where a machine is involved, if there are two or more people involved, a charge of *conspiracy* to defraud will lie.

The second actually goes to the root – and the purpose – of section 1 of the CMA, and that is the deterrent effect on the commission of further crimes, like fraud. By making unauthorised access in itself a crime, the Law Commission felt that a person contemplating fraud may be deterred if even the preliminary conduct, i.e. accessing a computer without authority, might expose him to the authorities and make him vulnerable to an even greater range of convictions. The Law Commission further stated that some of the seemingly 'innocent' hackers who find interesting information in their target system may go on to commit fraud or cause further damage, unless there is an earlier stage at which they can be caught and convicted, i.e. a section 1 hacking offence. The Law Commission also gave some weight to the belief that 'nursery hackers' might actually at times constitute a smokescreen for a real fraud being perpetrated behind it.

---

[10] The Law Commission, **Computer Misuse (Working Paper no. 110)** (London: HMSO, 1988), at para. 3.9.

[11] *See* note 4, *supra*

[12] *See* note 4, *supra*, at para. 2.8

10.6.5 Liability of directors?

Another factor to bear in mind is the possibility that at some time in the future directors of companies may be held accountable to shareholders for damage caused, and financial loss suffered, by companies as the result of outside intervention or employee abuse of the company's computer systems. As shareholders become more vocal about holding directors accountable for all sorts of deeds and misdeeds that take place in companies, it is foreseeable that directors will be held to account for computer systems that 'go wrong'. Thus, there is a strong incentive for making sure that at least 'reasonable endeavours' are undertaken to ensure that systems are protected and that employees do not abuse them.

10.6.6 Civil aspects

One reason often cited by victims for not reporting incidents of computer crime is the lack of civil redress. It is one thing to punish an offender, but quite another to extract compensation for the crimes. There are several issues here:

- because proof in hacking cases is difficult to begin with, it may prove to be almost impossible to find liability against a hacker in a civil law suit;
- a finding of contributory negligence may be found if the plaintiff cannot offer proof of having implemented security systems;
- insurance for computer misuse is still a rarity.

10.7 PREVENTING COMPUTER CRIME: POLICIES

Repressive methods of prosecution do not solve all of the problems, especially if, as we've seen, companies are reluctant to report incidents of computer crime. Instead, companies should consider the proactive measures which are available to them to prevent, or at least stem the growth of, computer crime which may affect their organisations. In other words, the threat of criminal behaviour should be converted into a duty of care, a duty that those who deploy computer technology take on as an ethical commitment.

There are two main avenues which can be particularly effective:

- security measures;
- codes of conduct.

10.7.1 Security measures

Security measures cover not only computer crime, but all of the dangers which confront, or potentially confront, a company and its computer systems (i.e.

natural disasters, human error, hardware and software defects, etc.). Threats to the computer systems from outside can be dealt with by a variety of devices and procedures, many of which are familiar to you. Threats – or potential threats – to systems from within, i.e. by employees, also can be dealt with by a variety of measures.

10.7.1.1 Personnel selection policy
The first step is to ensure that the company has a considered and effective personnel selection policy. No longer is it safe to rope in whizz-kid programmers from off the street or even accept at face value the c.v. of a new finance director whose last place of employment was A-1 Junk Bond Dealers & Co. Limited. Because of the wide take-up and understanding of computers at all levels of employees and the challenge which all computer systems offer to the new techie, potential employees must be checked out very carefully. This means following up references as well as any suspicions you might harbour about the *real* nature of the candidates' expertise. For example, serving time as a teenager in a juvenile home for taking Dungeons and Dragons too seriously should give you a clue about a young programmer's ulterior motives! The same diligence should be exercised even at the higher levels, even if the candidate will be only an end user.

10.7.1.2 The employment contract
The employment contract (or terms and conditions of employment) is another important tool in the fight against computer misuse and abuse. Companies should consider spelling out in the employment contract, in very clear and explicit terms, the boundaries of any particular employee's authority with respect to the use of (parts) of the firm's computer systems; his or her responsibility in enforcing this policy with respect to his or her colleagues; and the procedures to be followed in the event that he or she suspects or uncovers abuse. In addition, ACAS recommends that employers should give all employees a clear indication of the types of misconduct, including computer misuse, which will result in dismissal without notice or pay in lieu of notice.[13]

---

[13] *See Denco Ltd. v. Joinson* [Nov. 1990] in which the Employment Appeals Tribunal endorsed a company's strict regime in dealing with computer abuse by employees. By doing so, the EAT put deliberate computer misuse on a par with theft, fraud and drunkenness in the workplace. Joinson, who wanted information to help his trade union official's position in bargaining with his employer, was found to have made a deliberate attempt to gain access to confidential information through the misuse of a password. The EAT decided that this was more than mere unauthorised access (in which case dismissal may or may not be justified), that it was gross misconduct which was 'serious enough to destroy the employment contract between the employer and the employee and make any further working relationship and trust impossible'. In cases of summary dismissal, then, care should be taken to ensure that the offending behaviour (the misuse) is tantamount to serious misconduct since it is unlikely that the courts will uphold summary dismissal for less serious behaviour (in the courts' eyes) such as professional incompetency.

It also should be noted that the decision in Denco is not inconsistent with the Computer Misuse Act itself, thus a criminal prosecution may still lie even if the company were found to have acted wrongly in summarily dismissing the employees.

Notice is an especially important element, particularly if something goes wrong and the company seeks to prosecute the employee-offender.

10.7.1.3 Training

Once the new employee actually joins, he or she should be given training on the secure use of systems during induction training. This should include general awareness of computer crime and misuse generally, as well as the organisation's policy on software piracy and reading other people's E-Mail. The new employee also should be instructed to change his or her password frequently, and to refer to the computer security manual (if one exists) from time to time. He or she also should be given a clear idea of how far his or her authority extends with respect to modifying the company's data and programs, otherwise a charge of unauthorised modification under section 3 of the Computer Misuse Act could be brought!

10.7.1.4 Divided authority

Another safeguard to consider is ensuring that the responsibility for and knowledge of the firm's entire computer operations are *not* entrusted to one person, no matter how small the installation. The first reason is obvious – the firm would be in an incredible mess should that person be hit by a bus or even want to go off on a holiday longer than four hours. The second reason is one related to security: no one person should know enough about the computer systems so as to be able to disable or destroy them on his own. We only need look at the recent case of the typesetter's computer operator who locked the system, preventing anyone but himself using it.[14]

10.7.1.5 Computer, information and data audits

Computer, information and data audits may prove to be another effective security measure, both in terms of detecting ongoing frauds and crimes and for assisting the company in formulating its information and computer security policy.

10.7.2 Codes of conduct

As computers take over as the main tool for gathering, collecting and

---

[14] Richard Goulden was a disaffected computer contractor who feared that the company would not settle his invoice for £2,275 in contracting fees. Goulden disabled the company's main workstation by installing a US Government-backed security device on the workstation without notifying anyone of the password. The device could not be broken by any expert. The firm went into liquidation because of Goulden's actions. Goulden was charged under section 3 of the Computer Misuse Act, but was conditionally discharged and levied a light fine – because the judge felt that his actions were at 'the very lowest end of seriousness'. There are two issues here which are relevant: (1) the 'security measure' issue– this is a prime example of why authority and control should not be entrusted to one person; and (2) the need to educate the judiciary which we discussed earlier – here it is evident that the judge did not understand or appreciate the havoc which abuse to computers can wreak.

disseminating information in almost every area of commerce, many trade, industry and professional organisations and associations have included in their codes of practice provisions relating to 'good practice' in the use of computer systems.

Such measures exist in the IT field itself. For example, many of the computer associations which exist mandate certain levels of training and certification for their members and will not admit members who do not meet these criteria. Information security, confidentiality and integrity are often among the issues addressed, either directly or indirectly.

Similarly, professionals such as accountants may include a statement about information handling in their accounting and auditing standards. While specific mention of computer crime is not often mentioned, there is a general duty of care regarding confidentiality, independence and competence imputed to members which, by logical extension, includes information processed by computers. Also, there is a growing trend for DP professionals and accountants to work together in setting standards in the use of IT for accountants and auditors.

In terms of the legal effect of codes of conduct, unless the organisation (and its code) is directly sanctioned or established by the national government, the code is not binding. However, it can be cited in evidence in court in respect of the standards of competence which one would expect from an accountant or IT professional, etc. with respect to the behaviour in question.

Governments, as major IT consumers, also can be of help here by supporting private sector action in framing its buying policies in a security conscious way and by implementing voluntary codes of conduct.

10.8 COMPUTER CRIME IN OTHER EC COUNTRIES: A BRIEF SUMMARY

The approach to computer crime varies across Europe. A brief summary of some of the crimes and the various national approaches to them will be useful in highlighting some of the issues which are of concern in those countries and which may affect the way you do business in them.

10.8.1 Hacking (unauthorised access)

Ireland appears to grant the broadest definition to hacking. In Ireland, someone is guilty of hacking if he or she operates a computer with the *intent* to gain access, whether or not access is gained. The approaches in Germany, Denmark and Portugal are similar to each other and to that in the UK, namely that unauthorised access is crime per se, but not if access is not gained. More restrictive approaches are found in Greece, France and the Netherlands (pending) which require violation of safety measures. In addition, French legislation also requires the commission of a fraudulent act. In Italy, legislation is still pending, but is likely to require breach of a security device and probably also will punish the illicit possession and dissemination of codes. In Belgium, simple unauthorised access is not punished; the only possibility is to apply the Penal Code which requires entrance into the building where the computer is located. No law at all exists in Luxembourg or Spain.

10.8.2 Unauthorised access with intent to commit some further crime

Unauthorised access with intent to commit some further crime takes in a variety of offences, depending on the particular Member State:

- theft of data;
- alteration of and damage to data;
- fraud;
- company and state secrets.

10.8.2.1 Theft of data

Theft of data is a crime in almost every country. In Denmark and the Netherlands, theft of data is a crime *per se,* i.e. there is no requirement as to security devices being present as there is in Germany. In Ireland, not only is unauthorised access punishable, but so too is the *intent* to commit some other crime. Pending legislation may be found in Italy where the legislature seeks to punish theft of data, and to punish the thief more severely if the theft was for gain, and in Luxembourg where the law is expected to cover theft and misappropriation. Portugal has taken a more restrictive approach: theft of data is punishable only if there is an attempt to obtain an illegal benefit from the unauthorised access. The law in Greece is two-pronged. The Greek criminal code contains a comprehensive list of crimes relating to theft of data which can be punished where there are security measures present. Otherwise, the traditional crime of theft of a document includes *any* device on which data are stored. Spain and France do not specifically mention theft of data in their criminal codes, and in Belgium, only traditional Penal Code offences of theft apply.

10.8.2.2 Alteration of and damage to data

Again, alteration of and damage to data is an offence in almost every member state. However, definitions of 'damage' and 'alteration' vary to include:

- elimination;
- modification;
- destruction;
- erasure;
- concealment;

- partial/total deletion;
- tampering with data processing systems, etc.

In Spain, Luxembourg, the Netherlands and Ireland (as well as in the UK), data manipulation and tampering are crimes *per se*, regardless of the intent. Ireland, though, goes one step further – possession of anything with *intent* is sufficient. France and Greece take a broader view still, and in addition to making data manipulation and tampering punishable, also make *entering* data an offence. In Germany, the law punishes alteration of data and interference with the database system, even if the user is able to use the data. The approach in Portugal and Denmark are similar. In Portugal, damage and complete destruction are punishable only if there is an intent to cause prejudice to others or to obtain an illegal benefit. In Denmark, punishment can be levied only if the suspect seeks to gain enrichment from his alteration of the data. Existing legislation in Italy contains no provision for punishing alteration of or damage to data, but pending legislation includes a list of actions that would be punishable. In the private draft bill before the legislature, alteration, withdrawal, addition, elimination and tampering of data and programs would be punishable; the Government draft bill adds violation, substraction and suppression of data. There is no explicit mention of alteration of or damage to data in Belgium.

10.8.2.3 Fraud
The commission of fraud through the use of computers is punished in the Netherlands, Luxembourg, Denmark, Greece, Portugal and Germany. Legislation is pending in Italy. In Belgium, it is treated as traditional fraud, while in Spain and Ireland there is no specific offence mentioned. In some countries, fraud charges can be brought only against offenders in high positions, not against keypunchers, programmers or operators, for example.

10.8.2.4 Company and state secrets
Theft of company and state secrets held in a computer system is mentioned in the legislation of Spain, Germany, Denmark, Greece and the Netherlands. It is mentioned in the laws of other Member States as well, but not in the context of information security *per se*.

10.8.3 Damage to computers and telecommunications equipment (sabotage)

Most sanctions attach where *property* has been violated. In the case of damage to telecommunications equipment, most legislation deals with damage to the public network, thereby seeking to protect the public interest.

10.8.3.1 Computer sabotage
Traditional criminal sanctions dealing with damage to property apply in Luxembourg, Ireland, the Netherlands, Belgium and Denmark. More specific

legislation can be found in Portugal, Spain and Greece where reference is made to 'computer sabotage': behaviour affecting or intending to affect the functioning of a computer as a whole. In Germany, similar acts are punishable only if they affect or intend to affect operations which are of *significant* importance for another plant, business or public authority. Pending legislation in Italy refers to sabotage of computers and telematic systems and violence directed towards objects, i.e. computers. Nothing specific is mentioned in France.

10.8.3.2 Damage to telecommunications equipment
Damage to telecommunications equipment is not mentioned in France, Portugal, Spain, Greece or Ireland. However, in Germany there is comprehensive legislation which covers both direct damage to and indirect interference (such as abstraction of electricity) with telecommunications equipment. Additionally, where damage is caused which affects the public interest (e.g. to the public telephone network) more severe sanctions attach. Legislation in other jurisdictions varies: in Belgium, only traditional criminal sanctions can be used against the destruction of moveable property; in Denmark, there must be interference of a public or general nature before sanctions can apply; and in Italy, where legislation is still pending, damage must be done to an 'object', e.g. a telematic system.

10.9 THE NEW TECHNOLOGIES: WILL LEGISLATION STIFLE DEVELOPMENT?

Real questions emerge as legislation becomes more and more intrusive in the domains of computers, data and information. While we welcome this legislation in the sense that we hope that it deters criminal behaviour and protects our rights to privacy and to our own data, we need to take care that this same legislation does not stifle technological development.

At the most basic level, we need to ensure that the requirement for security devices (in some countries as a prerequisite for making a computer misuse violation stick) does not result in devices being developed which are so effective that no one – including law enforcement authorities – can break through them.

The most interesting issues arise in the development of new technologies that actually, or are perceived to, threaten privacy.

Examples include itemised call charges on phone bills (so intrusive that French husbands complained bitterly that their wives would then be able to find out who their mistresses are) and road pricing systems (which could produce the same result, as the movements of any given car could be traced for reasons other than assessing road usage).

In other developments, the ability to translate text, film, pictures, sound and graphics into digital signals makes it possible to record every phone call, cash withdrawal and credit card transaction, and to make copies which are indistinguishable from the original.

Recently, Lotus Corporation abandoned a joint venture with the credit rating bureau, Equifax, because the object of the joint venture was the distribution of a database containing the consumer habits of more than 120 million American households. Former Lotus President, Mitch Kapor, has gone on record condemning the unauthorised access to computer systems but at the same time supporting civil liberties in respect of freedom of information in the domain of digital storage.

In the United States, there is a debate raging which can best be described as computer-related privacy vs. free speech. An organisation called the Electronic Frontier Foundation has been set up to protect First Amendment rights in the realm of computing and telecommunications technology as well as the rights of computer professionals.

A case which falls within this debate involves the seizure by the FBI of hard copies, computers, etc. which the FBI thought were used in playing the game, Gurps Cyberpunk. As it turned out, and as the FBI are suspected of knowing, that particular game is not played on computers. Critics of this particular action fear that the FBI are seizing computers and large quantities of media just to frighten individuals they suspect to be hackers, not to seek convictions. Seizure of these materials is very likely tantamount to prior restraint of speech, conduct which seriously contravenes the First Amendment of the United States Constitution.

10.10 CONCLUSION

The Computer Misuse Act in the UK is a first step towards regulating an extremely complex and difficult area. As computing becomes even more integrated with commerce and industry, I believe that legislation and regulation in each of the sectors in which computers are at issue (e.g. banking, professional services, medicine, etc.) will have to be modified to take into account computer crime, misuse and abuse. More fundamentally, governments will have to take a look at the entire realm of information and construct a legislative and regulatory scheme that recognises the economic value and cultural importance of information, be it in verbal, written, or machine-readable form. After all, we live in an Information Society.

11 A Structured Control Methodology to Aid Data Security

John Mitchell
Computer Audit Specialist Group, BCS

11.1 INTRODUCTION

Data security is often considered to be the area of ensuring that only correctly authorised people are allowed to read, update, or delete particular data items. This is a particularly myopic view as it ignores whether the data itself is correct in the first place. Security is really a sub-set of control and control itself is something that is used to help ensure data integrity. Access rights and associated permissions are simply areas of data integrity and therefore need to be considered as part of an overall control methodology.

Controls are sometimes considered to be a wasteful overhead which inhibit the efficient and economical operation of the system, but a moments reflection will show that they are an essential requirement if effectiveness is to be achieved. Without controls the manager has no means of ensuring that the information provided by the system is correct, or that its security has not been breached.

11.2 DEFINITION

My definition of control is 'something which modifies, or monitors, the behaviour of a system so as to make it predictable'. It is this predictability, at every stage of processing which provides the reliance which can be placed on the final output. A system without controls may well be efficient, but it is also unpredictable.

11.3 RESPONSIBILITY FOR CONTROL

Responsibility for control rests with management. Management have a responsibility to ensure that an organisation's operations are conducted in an efficient, effective and economical manner.

All levels of management are required to see that their operations are well controlled, but difficulty in achieving this goal may be experienced where the ground is unfamiliar, or where it enters another manager's domain. Modern computer systems, using advanced data processing techniques and which involve more than one user, present the dual problems of unfamiliar processes and multi-domain responsibility.

It is essential therefore, that consideration be given to the subject of control at an early stage in the design process, as subsequent retro-fitting of controls to meet management's requirements can be a time-consuming and costly exercise. One of the first steps required is to allocate responsibility for defining the controls to specific members of the project team.

Responsibility for controls internal to the computer system usually resides with the Information Technology department, while the external clerical and administration controls are the responsibility of the user(s). This may still leave a large gap; such as who designs the output report which will be used to both ensure that all the data was processed successfully and for subsequent reconciliation within the user department(s)? The project leader needs to be aware of this potential conflict and to allocate responsibility accordingly. Ideally, there should be a separate section in both the requirements specification and the detailed design document dealing with the control environment.

11.4 REQUIREMENTS FOR PERFECT SYSTEM BEHAVIOUR

Perfect computer system behaviour can only be guaranteed if at any moment there is a methodology for ensuring that the system uses the correct:

a)   data;
b)   programs;
c)   master files;
d)   operating procedures;
e)   clerical procedures;

and that each of these elements can only be used by suitably authorised people.

11.5 TERMINOLOGY

As with any science, that of control has its own principles and terminology; an understanding of which is essential if well-controlled systems are to be designed. The following paragraphs provide guidance on these issues.

11.6 TYPES OF CONTROL

There are six main types of control applicable to computer systems:

a) prevention;
b) detection;
c) correction;
d) continuity;
e) contingency;
f) change.

11.6.1 Prevention controls

As their name implies these controls are to prevent an undesirable event from occurring. Input validation controls are a good example of this, as are access controls to prevent an unauthorised user from getting into a system.

Preventing invalid data from getting into the system in the first place is one of the most effective mechanisms in avoiding the GIGO (garbage in, garbage out) syndrome. Areas to be considered include:

a) ensuring that only numeric data can be accepted for numeric fields;
b) checking that a master file record exists before accepting a transaction,
c) conducting range checks to detect suspect data.

Prevention mechanisms are the first line of defence and careful consideration should be given to their design. It is worth remembering, however, that validation requirements may well change and what is currently (say) an acceptable salary range check may need increasing to take account of inflation.

11.6.2 Detection controls

These controls can be considered the converse of their preventive cousins, in that they detect things which may have slipped the preventive net. An example would be where a utility program is used to transfer data from one system to another but without that data going through the receiving system's validation processes. If some invalid data were accidentally transferred, such as an incorrect allowance code, then this should be detected by the allowance calculation module in the receiving system when it tries to calculate allowances.

A further example would be where a control total is maintained to ensure that all valid data is added successfully to a master file. If the subsequent check does not tally with that predicted then either the data has been processed incorrectly, or the master file has become corrupted in some way.

Detection controls are the second line of defence and it is a sound principle never to assume that the data is correct, the user is authorised, or that previous stages have operated correctly.

11.6.3 Correction controls

These controls enable an incorrect situation to be remedied with accuracy and speed. If, for example, a detection control found that the master file was corrupted, then its associated correction control would permit the rapid use of the previous version and the automatic reprocessing of all transactions processed since then.

It is important to remember that the correction mechanism must provide adequate information for action to be taken. It is no good simply displaying a message on a master console saying 'unauthorised user detected' and expect the recipient to divine the access point.

11.6.4 Continuity controls

These controls prove that processing has moved successfully from one stage to another. They can be further broken down as program-to-program, run-to-run and system-to-system controls, but the principles remain the same. Primarily they should ensure that:

a) all data has been transferred in each case;
b) the correct version of the master file(s) was used.

Control totals should be calculated at each processing stage and transferred to subsequent stages for validating. Any errors detected are likely to be of a serious enough nature to warrant halting the processing, but once again it is important that full information is provided as to the nature of the detected error.

11.6.5 Contingency controls

These controls provide a safety net in the event of a catastrophic failure occurring. This may range from the complete destruction of the physical hardware, a failure of the master file media, a major program logic error, or the loss of the input data. Always assume that the worse possible case will happen and devise a plan to recover from that situation in the shortest possible time, commensurate with the cost of doing so and the value of the system to the organisation.

In some instances the contingency will be covered by plans which are already in existence, such as the loss of a data centre, but in others it will be necessary to specifically design them for the system. Do not assume that a manual fall back is possible, as in many instances it is simply not viable, due to lack of manpower, or the geographical dispersion of the people concerned. Remember, the reason that the system was requested in the first place was probably to save on manpower.

11.6.6 Change controls

Any sort of change to a system is full of risk and it is a truism that most thing go wrong when an amendment is made to something which has been running successfully. The risk is well appreciated by computing professionals and there are often strict procedures to govern changes to computer programs. These controls often require authorisation before an amendment is made and its subsequent release into the production environment.

What about the data? Modern computer systems often use tables of data to define the processing that will take place, or have key data items, such as a VAT rate, which may affect every transaction in the system. Change control here is as important as change control over the code.

In some urgent cases, however, such as overnight payroll processing, it may be necessary to make a change to the table data without going through the pre-authorisation procedure. Where this happens be especially vigilant for undesirable side-effects and certainly ensure that the change is post-ratified. All systems should clearly state under what circumstances post-ratification is acceptable and what the subsequent checking mechanism should be.

11.7 CONTROL CONCEPTS

The six control types described above are all in fact a mix of only five different control concepts:

a) batching;
b) matching;
c) one-for-one;
d) totalling;   These are really just derivatives
e) check digit.   of the batching concept.

Indeed, if we accept the fact that (d) and (e) are simply derivatives of (a), then we only need to consider three main control concepts from which all the others are derived. This not only helps simplify the methodology, but also helps in classifying the various controls that may be found and whether they are likely to be effective for a particular error condition.

These concepts are explained below.

11.7.1 Batching

This is where items of related data are grouped together to ensure that nothing has been lost, changed, or added. Important numeric field(s) of data are totalled to provide a checksum which can be validated by the program. This is entered onto a 'batch header' which will also usually contain a count of the items in the batch (number of documents) as an added safeguard.

The program will test to ensure that the number of items processed and the total on the batch header agree with its own calculations. This ensures that no items have been lost or added and that the data in the significant field(s) has been transcribed correctly. If the test fails then all the data in the batch should be rejected, as the program cannot tell in which item the error exists.

The batching concept also covers the use of totals and check digits which are discussed later.

Batching is a powerful prevention and detection control mechanism but:

a) it is not suitable for checking alphabetic data;
b) compensating errors in a batch (i.e. -10 in one field being negated by +10 in another) will not be detected;
c) if the control total itself has been calculated incorrectly (a common error), then a valid batch of data will be rejected; and
d) it is not suitable for real-time systems, where data may be received and entered as single items.

For these reasons it may be more appropriate to use either matching or one-to-one.

11.7.2 Matching

This concept requires the matching of the incoming data with a code, or item, that is already on file; an example would be matching the stock item number from an issue sheet with a stock number on the stores master file. If the stock numbers cannot be matched then the incoming item would be rejected. A similar test could be done to check for a valid user identification and associated password.

The advantages of this technique are:

a) alphabetic items can be tested for existence;
b) items can be checked singularly, which is an advantage where real-time systems are concerned;
c) items can be tested, and if necessary rejected, at a very early stage in the processing cycle.

This last advantage is a very important superiority over the batching concept which may allow an incorrect item to travel as far as the update stage before it is rejected.

There is, however, one major disadvantage to the use of matching, and that is where the item to be matched does not yet exist on a master file as the incoming item is itself the creation record. In this case it may be necessary to use the check digit concept to ensure that the access key is created correctly.

11.7.3 One-to-one

A common problem associated with the above techniques is that they cannot prevent an unauthorised, but otherwise correct, transaction from being input into the system where real-time input from a terminal is concerned. For this reason, and where particularly important transactions are concerned, it may be better to use one-to-one checking.

This concept can be likened to checking your bank account against your cheque stubs. You expect to find one, and only one, transaction for each cheque and for the values to agree. Checking of this nature is laborious and it can only be used successfully where the transaction rate is low, as otherwise concentration will waver and mistakes may still go undetected.

If it is allied with statistical sampling, however, it can be a powerful post-input control for checking the input to real-time systems, and it may be useful to build a suitable statistically valid sampling routine of this nature into the system at the design stage. This would provide user management with a small, but valid, list of data for checking on a one-to-one basis.

11.7.4 Totalling

Totalling is really another form of batching, but in this case the data items are not necessarily physically grouped together and may be spread over a file. Totalling is often used to ensure that all accepted data is passed accurately between processing stages and that master files have not become corrupted.

This is especially important for systems where master file records may only be processed infrequently, such as a pensions system, as the loss or corruption of a record may otherwise go undetected for years. For systems of this nature it may be necessary to design special programs which can be run outside the normal processing schedule to check that nothing has been corrupted.

11.7.5 Check digit

The check digit approach can also be likened to batching and totalling, but in this case it is used to check the validity of a particular field. The 'batch' comprises the individual characters which make up the field and the check digit is the checksum of those characters. In this instance, however, the checksum is not usually a straight addition of the individual characters but a mathematical algorithm which helps to avoid the compensating error problem identified earlier.

The check digit concept helps to ensure that important master file access keys, such as stock numbers, are created correctly. Once created they themselves can be used to validate incoming data by using the matching concept.

One disadvantage is that the check digit has to be calculated prior to input and, as is the case with batching, it may be calculated incorrectly and thus lead to the rejection of what is otherwise a valid item. One way to mitigate against this is to use a special program to calculate the check digits of all potential input items and make this available to the user.

11.8 DIFFERENT DATA TYPES

The level of control which will be applied to different data items will, to a large extent, be determined by whether they are classified as being either standing or transaction data.

11.8.1 Standing data

Standing data items are defined as those items which tend to change infrequently and which themselves may affect many other items; an example would be a VAT rate. The importance of standing data from a control point of view is that if it is incorrect by even a small amount it can have a disproportionately large effect, due to it being applied against many transactions passing through the system. Take the VAT example; if the rate were held as 14% instead of 15%, then the 1% difference would be applied to many thousands of invoices, each of which would have the VAT incorrectly calculated. Correcting the actual error may be simple, but sorting out the results of the error would be extremely expensive.

11.8.2 Transaction data

Transaction data is that data which is transient in a system, such as the hours worked in a week by an individual employee. If that data item is incorrect, then only a single calculation will be wrong, as against the several thousand in the previous example.

Although it is essential to ensure that both standing and transaction data is correct, it is more important to ensure that the standing data is accurate, due to the more wide-ranging consequences.

11.9 COMPUTER APPLICATION CONTROL STAGES

When designing the control regime for a computer system it is useful to consider the system as having up to six processing stages:

a) input;
b) processing;
c) output;
d) program-to-program;

e) run-to-run;
f) system-to-system.

Not all systems will have all the stages and the stages themselves may consist of many modules, but most will have at least the first three stages mentioned above.

11.9.1 Input stage

This is one of the most important, as errors detected at this stage can be prevented from entering the system. This is often known as the data validation stage, where the input is validated against certain pre-determined rules, in order to avoid the GIGO syndrome mentioned earlier.

The prime requirements are that data should be complete, accurate, timely and not duplicated. It is likely that a mix of internal and external controls will be required in order to achieve this. Indeed, a mix of techniques is not unusual, but care must be exercised in order to avoid giving an illusion of control, by simply using every concept, without giving due regard to what is intended.

Which particular control concepts are applied will be determined to a large extent by the type of system, so it is worthwhile analysing whether it will be processing batches of data, in which case the use of the batching concept will be applicable, or whether it will be processing individual items, which will imply the use of matching, or one-to-one techniques.

11.9.2 Processing stage

Once transactions have entered the system it is important to ensure that they are processed correctly. In the majority of cases this will involve passing them from one program to another, changing a master file and generating output. The processing stage will often involve the transformation of the original input into something which may not be easily recognised as being related to it (e.g. a number of separate items will be transformed into a single total). The use of counts and totals to provide a trail will usually be appropriate.

11.9.3 Output stage

Totalling is again relevant as a control at the output stage. If bills were being produced, for example, the system could calculate the number and value of the bills produced. The user would then be able to check whether he has received that number and whether the value was within the range he expected.

Consideration should also be given to output retention requirements. Financial legislation often requires that records be held for six years, while Health and Safety statutes can impose retention periods of up to thirty years.

Where and in what form the records will be filed and how they will subsequently be accessed, should form part of the control considerations.

11.9.4 Program-to-program

The most appropriate form of control to ensure that transactions have been successfully transferred between programs is likely to involve the counting of different record types and the totalling of significant numeric data fields. These control records can be maintained as separate records, or fields, which can be tested by the program logic to ensure that nothing has been lost or corrupted.

For example, if the control record on a file created by a previous program indicated that it had processed 2,500 records with a total value of £300,000, then the receiving program would expect to process a similar amount.

11.9.5 System-to-system

These controls are similar to those used for program-to-program, except that in this case the data is leaving the boundaries of one system and entering another. A control report should always be produced showing what has been transferred and the receiving system should perform logic tests on the transferred file to ensure that everything has been received.

11.10 PLACEMENT OF CONTROLS

Controls do not always have to reside within the application system itself. In fact there are four possible places for controls:

a) within the application logic (i.e. in the programs);
b) within the application's operating environment (i.e. in the Operating System, DBMS, TPMS, etc.);
c) outside the operating environment but within Information Technology (i.e. database administration, network control, etc.);
d) outside the application (i.e. user clerical controls).

In-depth control is usually far better than putting all the controls in one place and some controls are more effective and efficient than others. For example, if access to data can be restricted by the teleprocessing monitor, then it would seem sensible to use that rather than to encode the access control within the application. Specific validation measures, on the other hand, are usually far better if coded into the application logic.

What is required is an overall assessment as to the level of control required and where it will reside. A matrix should be constructed showing the level of control for each data item, where it should be placed and which control concept is considered to be relevant. This will not only ensure that control is not neglected but will also highlight over-control which is wasteful and inefficient.

11.10.1 Clerical controls

To expect a new computer system to be implemented without it affecting the control environment of the system it is replacing is naive, and yet the external controls are often neglected until after the system has gone live. These external controls are, however, as important as those within the application in that they often provide the long-stop against program logic or operational errors.

11.11 THE MANAGEMENT TRAIL

The complexity of modern business systems often means that data is transferred and transformed many times during its conversion into records and information. This can make it difficult, or indeed impossible, to trace a transaction back to its source unless special consideration is given to the problem at the design stage. This tracing concept is often referred to as the audit trail, and because of its name it is often thought that it is there at the demand of, and for the sole use of, the auditors. This is not the case, and in order to remove this misconception it is now more often referred to as the management trail, as this makes it quite clear that it is there for management control purposes.

The prime purpose of the management trail is to enable the tracing of those transactions which cause a change to occur to the data already in the system, or which trigger processing leading to variable output. It is not usual, except in certain high security systems, to require the trail to be extended to enquiry transactions. For example, it would be necessary to be able to trace the origination of a transaction which changed a person's pay record, or the value which was entered to trigger a print showing what the effect would be of a particular percentage pay increase, but it would be unusual to require the tracing of an enquiry against a stock record.

With real-time systems, the management trail may be provided for automatically by the Teleprocessing Monitor or the Database Management System as part of the recovery mechanism, but in other cases it may be necessary to code the required logic into the application.

The control matrix mentioned earlier could be extended to identify those transactions which necessitate the requirement to be traced back to their source. This would ensure that consideration is given to the trail at the design stage.

11.12 TIMING OF CONTROL

Although prevention is often better than cure, it may be inappropriate to always use prevention controls in computer systems. Pre-authorisation of input (which is a prevention control) is not effective where real-time systems are concerned as it is possible to enter a transaction at a terminal without the need for a paper document. In such a situation, not only is pre-authorisation useless as a control, but it may well introduce inefficiency, in the form of delays, into the system. This is a prime example of an unsuitable control being selected, but what is worse is that it may well give an illusion of control.

For real-time systems it may be more relevant to use a post-authorisation form of control, based on the requirement to compare transactions entered into the system against the source documents, but after processing has been completed. Where high volumes are the norm it may be sensible to produce a statistically valid sample of the transactions for checking purposes.

The time period between a prevention control failing and a detection control being triggered is known as the exposure window. The size of this window is an indication of the risk that the organisation is willing to accept in having incorrect data in a particular system, or having its correct data exposed to a potential misuse.

The timing of control is therefore something else that needs to be considered at the design stage.

11.13 BALANCING OF CONTROL

It is as easy to over control a system and make it inefficient and uneconomic as it is to under control it and make it ineffective. The balance is not easy to achieve, but it is far easier to get it correct at the design stage than to sort out a number of conflicting controls after the system has gone live.

The four things that need to be balanced are:

a) system efficiency;
b) system effectiveness;
c) economy of operation;
d) risk of exposure.

The main trade-offs to be considered are efficiency v. effectiveness and economy v. risk. These will be different for each system.

11.14 DOCUMENTING OF CONTROLS

Controls within a system should be documented like any other piece of processing. Ideally, they should be clearly specified in separate sections of the requirements and detailed design documents, using the framework described below.

11.14.1 Introduction

There should be a short introduction providing an indication as to the value and/or importance of the items processed and the use that will be made of the output. This is to enable the subsequent control design to be evaluated in context.

11.14.2 Access restrictions

The introduction should be followed by a brief overview as to whether the system will operate in real-time or batch mode, as this will affect the control environment. The required degree of protection from unauthorised access to the system should be stated, together with any requirements of the Data Protection Act.

11.14.3 Input control

The next section should describe how completeness and accuracy of input will be controlled. Each of the inputs should be described with its relevant validation requirements, the action which is to be taken on failure and how correction will be achieved.

Standing and transaction data should be identified and those inputs which will cause a significant change to the system should be flagged as candidates for the management trail.

11.14.4 Processing control

The method of ensuring that all accepted items are correctly processed through each system stage should be defined, including ensuring that the correct version of the master file is used and that there has been no corruption of its contents; this is especially important where records may lie dormant for long time periods. Particular attention should be given to data which crosses system boundaries as it may be necessary to modify the receiving system to ensure that control is not lost.

11.14.5 Output control

Finally, control over the output should be dealt with, detailing how it will be checked for accuracy and including any retention and security requirements.

11.15 CONCLUSION

Well-controlled systems are essential to the successful operation of an organisation. Data security is only one aspect of the total control environment and it needs to be balanced against efficiency and effectiveness consideration. It should be remembered that control is a managerial and not a technical responsibility. The technical aspects are simply the implementation of management's requirements.

12 Securing your PC

Alex McIntosh
PC Security

12.1 SOME RECENT HEADLINES

Computer security has been very much in the news lately, sparking off headlines and quotations like the following:

- 'Computers lack security' (US National Academy of Sciences, December 1990).

- 'Security on laptops still lax in UK firms' (*PC Business World*, January 1991).

- 'People don't keep sensitive information on laptops' (City stockbroking house).

- 'In terms of security, we don't have any rules' (Consultant with large accounting firm).

- 'LAN security at risk from increased personnel skill' (*PC Week*, January 1991).

12.2 THE RISE OF THE PC

In the early 70s, Peter Drucker identified information and timeliness of information as two key company assets. The provision of appropriate security for these assets is of major importance to industry, commerce and government.

A senior executive in a major UK company recently highlighted the growing importance of PCs saying, 'I am not sure that we will buy a mainframe computer again. We won't get rid of what we have, but today it performs only one role, that of a massive file server'.

What he was indicating was that, as time went on, more and more of the real IT work would be processed on PCs, and that as those PCs were connected in LANs, the great majority of the computing power, and spending on computing power, would be on PCs and workstations. Hence, at any one time, large amounts of the company's information would reside on PC hard disks, under the control of individual users.

PCs are no longer business toys. They are powerful computing devices capable of processing vast amounts of information, in volumes which just a few years ago would have required mainframe capacity.

12.3 DATA SECURITY

Data security has been part of mainframe culture for twenty years or more. The rules were established many years ago, and a manager is appointed in most companies to ensure the integrity of all data held on mainframes.

The same cannot be said of the PC. Not only have PCs encouraged a huge growth in the number of computer users since the IBM PC was announced in the UK in January 1983, but much of the data stored is just as sensitive as that stored on mainframes, with few, if any, security rules or devices.

Everyone agrees that computer crime exists, but putting a figure on the extent of the crime is difficult. Michael Colvin MP, was quoted recently as saying 'computer crime is costing UK industry an estimated £400 million to £1 billion every year'. Colvin's Computer Misuse Bill contains several credible aims, but one major factor has yet to be considered. How do you catch people who misuse computers, especially PCs? Bear in mind that the other widely quoted statement is, 'It is estimated that 90% or more of computer crime is perpetrated by employees'.

If your PC or laptop is stolen, you can replace the machine itself on insurance. But the real problem is the loss or misuse of the data, especially if it consists of confidential information on your company's business plans.

PCs are also vulnerable to other threats, including the risk of computer viruses, and the risk of loss of data due simply to bad user practices.

The technology exists today to remove or greatly reduce these risks: computer hardware and software devices offer varying levels of access control, protection from computer viruses and automatic back-up of files.

What is more, the cost of that technology is very much less than the cost of recovery: in a recent example of misuse, where a virus was introduced into a number of systems, the technical support staff took several weeks to recover the systems. Costly, and a diversion of valuable resources.

12.4 WHY IS DATA SECURITY FOR PCs IMPORTANT?

Information Technology is critical to the conduct of modern business. As more and more company business is carried out on PCs, individual PC users have built databases containing information that previously resided on mainframe systems under the control of the IS manager, or in filing cabinets, and desks, much of it controlled by secretaries and administrators. It is now concentrated in one location, on one system, and, if unprotected, is available to unauthorised users.

This is not just a problem for the large corporations, although it is clearly difficult to have a clear idea of what is held on two or three thousand PCs. The most common complaint is, 'We don't know what we have (i.e. how many and what type of systems), and we don't know who uses them, or for what'.

In smaller companies, it is quite likely that a large proportion of the information assets will be held on PCs. If these PCs are stolen, changed or destroyed, such companies could lose many of their assets, and may also lose their competitive position.

12.5 THE SIZE OF THE PROBLEM

The size of the problem is clear from the facts outlined below.

12.5.1 Number of systems installed

There has been a tremendous growth in the number of PCs installed over the last eight years. Industry watchers reported 740,000 units shipped in 1987, 1 million in 1988, and over 1.1 million in 1989, making almost 3 million in three years. The forecast for 1991 is 1.5 million.

12.5.2 Power and performance

The PC of today is the mainframe of yesterday. Those mainframes you locked up so carefully five years ago are now on everyone's desk, and together with the power of application software delivered by the industry, they represent a formidable array of computing power.

And the rate of change of technology is not abating in any way. Tomorrow's PC or workstation will have a faster processor, more data storage capacity, more communications capability, and more powerful software.

12.5.3 Growth in risk

Freedom of access, portability, and user knowledge all increase the threats to data stored on the PC.

Over the last eight years, the average British employee has lost all fear of keyboards, and become comfortable with computers. The individual who wants to gain entry does not have to be a computer professional to hack into a PC's files. With a little time, and some knowledge of DOS, he can steal, copy, destroy and modify data, and get away with it.

12.6 SOLUTIONS

If your employees are careful, honest, and not inquisitive, establishing a number of rules may help to deliver a certain level of security.

The laptop computer stolen from the car of an RAF officer in December 1990 highlighted the risks of portable computers, with the information contained therein available to the thief, or to anyone who purchased it from him.

A more striking example of the extent of the threat involved a prominent New York company which had a well documented policy to prevent the introduction of a virus onto any of the corporate PCs. All diskettes brought in from the outside were analysed by an isolated PC running virus detection software; any diskettes that were found to contain a virus were destroyed, and only 'clean' diskettes were allowed to be used on other computers. This procedure routinely discovered infected diskettes and saved the company from a virus attack on numerous occasions.

One morning, several PCs would not work properly because they had been infected with a virus overnight. The next day several additional PCs were infected. This mysterious virus continued to infect random PCs for several weeks. Ultimately, it was discovered that the cleaning staff, who came in during the night, had a game on a diskette that they would insert into any available PC. The diskette contained a virus that would infect the hard disk whenever the game was played.

These examples show that a company may not be able to control all of the actions of all of the people who have access to its PCs, but it can control what is done on them.

12.7 USING TECHNOLOGY TO EXERCISE CONTROL

Now that it is almost universal practice to store business-critical data on PCs, the main risks that companies face are deliberate theft, destruction or unauthorised change, and accidental destruction through bad practice – i.e. through the users' lack of knowledge of, or training in, the use of the technology and simple rules.

Because not all PCs are used in this way, it is not always necessary to use access control devices or top of the range technology. However, experience suggests that as user awareness of the risks grows, so does the awareness that even accidental destruction or change to data affects the user's ability to perform his allotted task.

Initially, the real need is to control access to the PC through the keyboard. Thereafter, as the value of the data increases (or the threats to it increase), you can build in multiple features, such as encryption and audit trail, smartcards and swipe badge readers, and voice and signature recognition devices.

Within this section, we need to consider the following:

- access control
- function
- access control to PC
- access control to files and applications
- access control to devices – 'A' drive, comms port
- encryption
- audit trail
- ease of use
- ease of administration.

The importance of ease of use cannot be stressed enough: when users have had unlimited and uncontrolled access to their system, they don't take too kindly to new rules.

Ease of administration becomes particularly important as large LANs are developed: it has already become a major requirement to be able to develop and change user profiles centrally.

Companies which have few or no rules need some form of handy, easy-to-use reference card. One such card, developed by a major assurance company, was the spearhead for a user awareness program which has had very beneficial results. The card identifies the do's and don'ts for both users and managers, and offers good practical advice. It contains information on what to do in an emergency, where to get help, the Data Protection Act, computer viruses, and so on. A few months after this user awareness program, all employees were able to put some value on the cost to the company of a breakdown in security, and understood how the value of their data was constantly expanding.

12.8 GOVERNMENT CERTIFICATION

In 1990, the DTI and the Communications-Electronics Security Group (CESG) established a national security evaluation and certification scheme for IT systems and products.

The scheme aims to enable users to establish greater confidence in the security of their IT products and systems by:

- providing industry, commerce and government with the means to obtain a security evaluation of IT systems and products;

- providing a basis for the international mutual recognition of certified evaluation results.

Evaluation under the scheme is carried out by commercial concerns known as Commercial Licensed Evaluation Facilities (CLEFs), under licence from a Certification Body staffed jointly by the DTI and the CESG. Products and systems which are successfully evaluated will be issued a certificate by the Certification Body.

This scheme was established on a pilot basis to supersede that currently operated by the CESG and previously planned by the DTI. It became fully operational in March 1991. The Information Technology Security Evaluation Criteria (ITSEC), which provide the basis for evaluation under the scheme, were developed by the UK, France, Germany and the Netherlands as a harmonisation of existing criteria.

A conference sponsored by the European Commission to discuss ITSEC took place in Brussels on 25-26 September 1990. It is expected that it should help ensure that these criteria reflect a truly international consensus, and provide schemes which operate the criteria with a good prospect of achieving mutual recognition.

The premise is that evaluation, conducted against recognised criteria (ITSEC), by a competent third party (CLEF), licensed and certified by an independent organisation (the Certification Body) provides a significant assurance (or confidence) in the security features provided by IT systems and products.

In the past, the CESG and the DTI have published works (CESG Memoranda, DTI Green Books) aimed respectively at government and commercial security needs. This joint initiative establishes a new national scheme to adequately address both government and commercial interests in a single, coherent approach.

Two operational evaluation facilities already exist, established under the old CESG scheme. These are Logica Space and Defence Systems Ltd, and Secure Information Systems Ltd. These facilities have been re-licensed under the new scheme.

Documentation for the scheme and further information may be obtained from either of the following:

The Certification Body	or	Computer Security Branch
UK IT Security Evaluation		Information Technology Division
and Certification Scheme		Department of Trade and Industry
Room 2/0804		Kingsgate House
Fiddlers Green Lane		66-74 Victoria Street
Cheltenham GL52 5AJ		London SW1E 6SW
Tel: 0242 221491 x 4377		Tel: 071 215 2735

12.9 SOFTWARE PIRACY

Company executives should also be concerned about software piracy. Two organisations, the Business Software Alliance (BSA) and the Federation Against Software Theft (FAST), have launched a series of police raids designed to deter large companies from illegally copying programs.

Recent UK figures show that illegal copying costs software manufacturers £300 million a year. This is especially striking when you consider that this money would otherwise be spent on research and development.

In 1990, a poll carried out on behalf of FAST found that over half of all senior managers using PCs copy software illegally. One in three said their company had no control over software duplication.

Bob Hay, chief executive of FAST says, 'If your company finishes up in court it doesn't really matter whether it is through ignorance or not.' What you are putting at stake is not only a considerable amount of money but also your company reputation. Mr Hay goes on to say that problems are often caused by 'a lack of strong managerial direction.'

In a number of companies today, illegal software copying is a dismissable offence.

12.10 CONCLUSIONS

Information Technology has become the vital backbone of every successful business. However, there are numerous threats to the security of these systems, particularly those based on PC/LANs. Deliberate damage, fraud and straightforward human error present a constant worry to management.

In today's business world it is vital for senior management to understand the degree of reliance placed on information systems, and the risks to which they are exposed. Effective management of IT security risks requires an understanding of the assets that require protection, their vulnerability to threats and the adequacy of existing controls. Obtaining this understanding is a rigorous process, requiring knowledge of the business as well as IT and security skills. Ensuring that adequate levels of protection are in place requires clear policies and management commitment.

It is in your interests to know the answers to the following questions. How secure is the information held on your PCs? How much at risk are you from the hacker or the casual browser; from accidental loss or destruction of data by an employee; from lack of conformity with the Data Protection Act; from illegal practices in software copying?

12.10.1 A few words of advice

A review of your company procedures on data security may establish that they are firmly in place for mainframe systems but inadequate or non-existent policies for PCs and laptops.

In this case, you can take a number of actions:

1. understand how your PCs are being used;

2. ensure that responsibility for the security of all corporate data is assigned to the appropriate person;

3. extend your data protection strategy to include PC users;

4. use awareness programmes to educate and train users in data protection;

5. assign responsibility for the implementation of a company-wide data protection strategy to line management; and

6. ensure, by auditing, that your strategy is implemented.

A number of methodologies are available that go some way to helping companies to establish the risks.

In addition to these, we have developed what we call the 'Minimum Corporate Standard' for personal computer security. It is designed to help organisations implement a minimum level of PC security immediately, whilst providing end-users, through a questionnaire, with a simple means of assessing what additional PC security function they may require to meet their individual application and data security needs.

In the past, users have been confused by being given product descriptions without any indication of why they might need the various features. This questionnaire takes a completely different approach. Each feature is described individually without any mention of products and the users given an indication of why they might need the feature.

The reasons why users might need any of these additional features are explained in non-technical language so that they can select the security features appropriate to their individual needs and not incur the costs of features that are unnecessary. This only works when you have access to a full range of products.

12.10.2 A final word

In late 1989, Peter Wild of Coopers & Lybrand in New York said in a paper in the US *EDP Auditor*, 'Just as, for example, you cannot buy a new car today without seat belts, perhaps you should not be able to buy a computer without access control'.

Peter was a few years early. But we can safely say today that a number of microcomputer companies have recognised this fact, and will soon be shipping security products in the same way that today they ship DOS.

Printed and bound by CPI Group (UK) Ltd, Croydon, CR0 4YY

21/10/2024

01777086-0013